THE
LITTLE MONK

BY HARRY FARRA
drawings by Christopher Fay

PAULIST PRESS
New York and Mahwah, N.J.

Library of Congress Cataloging-in-Publication Data

Farra, Harry.
    The little monk / Harry Farra.
        p.   cm.
    ISBN 0-8091-3356-3 (paper)
    1 Spiritual life—Christianity. 2. Prayer—Christianity. 3. Parables.
I. Title.
BV4501.2.F32   1994
242—dc20   94-14506
                                                                  CIP

Published by Paulist Press
997 Macarthur Boulevard
Mahwah, NJ 07430

Printed and bound in the
United States of America

Contents

ACKNOWLEDGEMENTS

"The Wish of Manchan of Liath," in "The Responsibility of Glory" chapter is from Kenneth Hurlstone Jackson's *A Celtic Miscellany* and is used by permission of Routledge in England.

The idea of "a thin place," in the chapter "The Fellowship of Faith," was sparked by an article of David P. Jones in the *Trinity* newsletter of the Episcopal Diocese of Pittsburgh, June, 1989.

I'm indebted to the many saints and other writers whose thoughts, sometimes specifically cited, sometimes not, are woven into the tapestry of this book.

I want to thank my colleague, Suhail Hanna, for his many suggestions and unwavering support of me in all of my writings, including this one.

A constant inspiration has been the Aberdeen Prayer Group, a small core of faculty and staff who meet every Wednesday in an inconspicuous corner of the campus for faithful prayer.

I owe a long-overdue debt to Gloria Meece who took me aside when I was a teenager and set me off on the journey of prayer.

My thanks also go to my secretary, Paula Schmolly, for typing the first draft and, along with Brenda Lichius and Robb Tweddell, answering all my how-do-you questions about the computer.

Libraries are often a writer's first tool. I appreciate the constant aid of the various staff members of McCartney Library at Geneva College.

I am indebted to my friend, Christopher Fay, for a superb job of artwork for this book.

Lastly, I want to thank the helpful people at Paulist Press, and, in particular, two persons. My competent editor, Karen Scialabba, encouraged me greatly by caring as much for my manuscript as I do. Her wisdom in many intricate details of the manuscript vastly improved the book. Also, I owe untold gratitude to Father Lawrence Boadt who saw something more in the little monk's story than even I did in writing it.

DEDICATION

This book is dedicated first of all to my family: to my children, Heidi and Kirk, who have always been interested in "Dad's writings," and to my wife, Vonnie—friend and partner, guide and companion—who has always been there for me.

This book is also dedicated to the memory of two very close friends who passed away during the period of the writing of the book: John Montini and Ellie Heddendorf.

The book is further dedicated to my rector at St. Stephen's, in Sewickley, Pennsylvania—Mike Henning, who knows what it is to go through "the dark night of the soul, and to come out with serenity and light."

Finally, the book is dedicated to all those true believers who know that this is not a book about monks and monasteries.

Good Friday
1994

"Next I saw seven trumpets being given to the seven angels who stand in the presence of God. Another angel, who had a golden censer, came and stood at the altar. A large quantity of incense was given to him to offer with the prayers of all the saints on the golden altar that stood in front of the throne; and so from the angel's hand the smoke of the incense went up in the presence of God and with it the prayers of the saints. Then the angel took the censer and filled it with the fire from the altar, which he then threw down on to the earth; immediately there came peals of thunder and flashes of lightning, and the earth shook."

Revelation 8:2-5
The Jerusalem Bible

1. The Strength of a Sickly Child

"**K**eep an eye on that boy," the doctor said. "He's a sickly one for sure."

His mother had brought him down to London for a complete physical examination.

For most of his early years, the child had fought one illness after another. Lately, his mother had been worried about his strange, lingering cough, so had decided to take him to the city for a full set of tests with the noted doctors there.

The carriage that brought them to London had rumbled through the misty moors of countryside England and then clattered down the cobblestone streets of the great city.

"Will it hurt?" the boy asked his mother as they traveled along.

"If it does, it will be for your own good," his mother answered, pressing his hand into hers.

He always puzzled over things that somehow hurt for your own good.

The doctor they met was busy but kindly.

"The cough will go in time with the medicine I'll give you," he announced with authority. Then quietly to the boy's mother he said, "He's not very strong. You'll have to watch him with a keen eye." He checked the boy over from nose to toes. She was glad she had washed his ears.

"He's worried us often. He seems so pale and listless, so

1

"Mother, why did God make me so weak?"
he asked, breaking the silence.

small for his age," the mother replied. "He's such a sad one, too—so melancholy at times."

On the ride home, after all the pokes and prods of the doctor, the boy slumped silently in a dark corner of the covered carriage.

"Mother, why did God make me so weak?" he asked, breaking the silence.

"Because he wants to give you his strength."

"But all the other children tease me and call me names like Cry-baby and Shy-baby."

"That's because they think you're weak and they're strong."

"But I am weak, mother, I am weak," he exclaimed.

"Only because you think so," his mother answered, hoping to end the matter.

He didn't want to tell her that town bullies also punched him in the shoulders and stomach quite often.

"When will God make me strong?" he asked.

"He's started already, but it will take time. You may have to suffer much first."

He did not like the sound of the words, "suffer much." Why does it always seem to involve something unpleasant when grownups tell children the truth? he wondered.

"How will God make me strong?" he asked.

"I don't know, but it will probably be in answer to prayer. Your grandfather always used to say: 'Every prayer has within it the seed of its own answer.' He always talked about praying without ceasing. I think if you find out what that means you will be the strongest person on earth."

In the year that Queen Victoria died, a hinge in history that swung the world into a strange new century, the boy came to the age for seeking a trade. His mother looked into an apprenticeship for her son with some local artisan in wood, iron, gold or pottery. They had no money for him to attend the university.

"Why don't you become a potter?" she asked, having narrowed down the choices.

"That's such delicate work. I don't know if I have the hands for it," he answered, looking at hands that were cold and frail, with no sign of artistry in them.

"You have good hands," she said, taking his hands in hers and kissing them and holding them up proudly.

"But will I be strong enough to please the master potter? Some of those pots are large and heavy. Don't they often pack several together in huge crates?"

"Someday, you will be a giant," she said as she pulled herself up as tall as she could, with her hands arched over her head, pretending to be the biggest giant ever. "Fe, fie, fo, fum—I smell the blood of an Englishman," she boomed out in a deep voice.

He laughed freely at this game they had often played when he was a young child.

"You *will* be a giant someday," she announced. "A gentle giant."

2. A Potter Made of Clay

"*A*nother ruined clay pot," exclaimed a worried apprentice in the potter's house.

Two potters sat at their wheels. One of them was a master craftsman and the other, so short his feet hardly touched the ground, was a beginner.

The apprentice sadly picked dobs of clay from between his fingers. No matter what he did, his pots cracked when fired in the kilns—every one of them.

The master, with endless patience, would lead the apprentice through the process again, step by step. The master's pots were pieces of art, known worldwide.

All day long the little learner would sit at his wheel shaping his pots. They always seemed to be like the master's. Yet, when he would fire the pots in the kiln slowly— ever so slowly—for hours on end, his pots would always develop cobweb-thin cracks.

Again the master showed him the ancient secrets of the clay. Still, his artless pottery all cracked under stress.

He was embarrassed to be in the same house with the master. Late that night he packed his belongings to leave. Holding his breath he crept to the door in order to sneak out. The floor creaked beneath him and aroused the master. The master called, "Where are you going?"

"I must leave," said the apprentice. "I cannot be like you."

In flannel night-shirt and floppy cap, the master shuf-

"He said a simple prayer..."

fled over to the young man and gently put his arm around his shoulder.

"Little one, the greatest lesson for you to learn is to be yourself. When you are you, your clay pots will respond to the touch of your hands," said the master.

"What am I doing wrong?" asked the apprentice.

"All you lack is patience, for patience is the conquering hero of all battles. Don't let time and emotion become your enemies. The rich and wealthy know for a fact that a little money at modest interest over a long period of time will bring a fortune. Wealth, they say, is the handmaiden of patience. Patience is acting as if there are no minutes and hours to worry about. You need to learn the patience of the acorn which finally grows into a mighty tree. Patience is the power to outwait defeat."

"I don't know if I have the gift," said the apprentice. "I'll never make a good clay pot. I'll never be a master craftsman. I'll never do great things in the world."

"Tomorrow you will begin anew," the master proclaimed. "Trying has its own rewards. As for greatness, it comes when you no longer seek it or need it."

That night a light fog, soft as angel's hair, floated in and across the land. Early the next morning before the sun had burned off the fog, the apprentice went out toward the shed where the discarded pottery lay. Piled high were the skeletons of broken, wasted and unfinished pots and vases, looking like some abandoned graveyard. He said a simple prayer, "Dear Father, you are the master potter. Show me how you do your work and I'll serve you all the days of my life. Amen."

The rest of that day, as his potter's wheel whirled with a fresh lump of clay, the apprentice worked his thin fingers into the rebel clay with love and zeal. He talked to the clay, encouraging it to come to life. Seven items he made that day, letting them dry for a day or so before patiently firing them in the hot kiln.

At the end of the third day, he carefully opened the iron door of the cooled kiln. He peeked in. The clay objects were cracked—all but one, that is. A small vase in the corner of the kiln was perfect in every respect.

Awed that God had answered his prayer, the little apprentice washed his hands in fresh, cold water. When the vase had cooled, he held it up to the light and turned it in his hands, inspecting every detail for any possible flaws. None! He saw the vase that he had made and said, "That's good." He glazed it the next day and, by the end of the week, placed it on the show table.

A customer slowly entered the door and looked over the assortment of vases and other pottery. When he saw the latest addition to the collection, he ran to examine it. "How beautiful," he exclaimed and bought the vase at a great price. "Who made this?" he asked.

The master potter pointed to the little apprentice who blushed and rocked nervously back and forth on the potter's bench.

3. The Calling

*A*lthough his reputation as a craftsman, an artisan, quickly spread throughout the land, the apprentice became uneasy and restless about this work. More and more, he came to realize that it was not to be a potter that he was called, but to be clay himself molded for other purposes by the Eternal Potter.

The young man, so moved by this realization, dedicated his life to enlarging his soul, to helping it grow like the tiny acorn. But the Holy Spirit, infinite in variety and surprise, had plans far greater than even the young man could imagine.

Like all young people, however, he, too, was subject to the rituals of doubt and the ceremonies of uncertainty.

Several weeks later, he left the potter's house and went to find his place in life. Day after day, he wandered the marketplace talking endlessly to shopkeepers, to vendors hawking their wares and to smelly fishermen.

He picked up a hundred items to handle, inspect and discuss with their owners. Once his eye caught a beautiful piece of cloth that would have made someone a handsome garment. As he examined the cloth, he was reminded of the words of Isaiah, "You have folded up my life like a weaver, who severs the last thread."

All the while, he was searching for some sign, some indication of where he might fit into the scheme of things and what might be God's plan for him in the world. He was young, eager to get on with his life and hopeful of

good things for himself. He had ached too long for meaning and purpose and direction in life. "Looking for one's
calling is like having a constant toothache," he told one
shopkeeper who had taken a few minutes to listen to him.
The young man held his jaw as if it were throbbing with
pain.

"Our God is unhurried and moves at a turtle's pace. He
sometimes has difficulty getting the attention of the restless ones so he can point the way," replied the shopkeeper.
"The young, standing at the edge of the future, are
painfully aware of the awesome weight of being."

One day, down near the docks, he saw an old barefooted monk, begging for food. Someone shoved into the old
monk's hands a few remains of fish, the heads and tails
that had been cut off for swill for pigs. The toothless monk
gummed a few nibbles and shared the rest with a colony
of hungry seagulls. He bowed his head in thanksgiving,
blessed the seagulls and then headed off to beg some
more.

The apprentice wondered at the sight of the beggar
monk and marked each move he made, like a child watching a caterpillar in autumn.

"I can't imagine anyone wasting his life like that," a
cynical vendor snarled. But, as the old monk passed by,
the young apprentice was drawn to his eyes, eyes that
were rings of shimmering fire on the outer edges and
pools of molten crystal farther in. Those compelling eyes
pulled the little apprentice deep into the very center of
them where he saw a strange thing, what he thought was
the image of a lamb on a hill.

He ran away and lost himself in the crowd. Later that
night as he tried to sleep, his dreams were punctured
again and again by the figure of the lamb on the hill. The
lamb was looking at him. This terrified him. He groaned
aloud in his sleep and turned his face to the wall.

"One day...he saw an old barefooted monk..."

Next day, at the south end of the marketplace, where the cheapest of goods were sold and traded, he ran across a booth marked "Dreams Interpreted." A dirty, ragged woman, part sage and part huckster, motioned to him.

He hesitated at first, then held out a coin which was snatched from his hand. She quickly hid the coin beneath her skirt, while he told her his dream. She studied his face, turned his hands over and over in her own and looked far into his eyes. Finally she said, "The lamb is on the hill, waiting for you—for you alone."

"What does that mean?" he asked, a little frightened.

The dream teller seemed very nervous and worried. "That's all I have for you. Doesn't it have any significance for you? Please leave. Go now."

He started to plead with her to tell him more, but she pushed open the tent door and urged him to leave. He was jostled and carried along by the crowd in the marketplace. All the sights, sounds and smells of that human sea whirled into a foam within him.

On his way, he again caught a glimpse of the aged monk, begging for his daily bread. He squinted hard at the monk, hoping that by shutting everything else out, he might be able to grasp the meaning of this monk. But a loud voice broke into his thought.

"What a great pity," a rich merchant said. "Aren't you glad that God hasn't called you to such a loathsome way of life?"

Suddenly, he knew. God *was* calling him to be a monk.

But he was afraid. He ran until tired and then found himself again in step with the ballet of the marketplace.

A little later, someone from the crowd bumped into him so hard that he spun around and came face to face with a stunning sight. A man had a rope tied around the neck of a lamb, leading it off silently to be slaughtered. The lamb looked at the young apprentice, but made no sound, no plea for help. The horrible scene exploded in his mind, splintering his thoughts into a thousand pieces: "The lamb is on the hill, waiting for you—for you alone."

A tremendous dread filled him. He felt as though his lunch was coming up. He grabbed his mouth and fled behind a woodworker's shop, where he fell on his knees in prayer. His spirit, spilling out all its sin and doubt, raced with abandon across the moat that led to the kingdom of living fire.

He surrendered himself fully to God and said, "Make me a monk, but do it gently."

4. A Life for God

*M*onths later, the little potter left the world behind to join a nearby monastery. His sole desire was to lose his life in the contemplation of God: to become a monk of prayer, a monk who could teach the world how to pray with the meekness of a lamb.

The day he left home his mother pressed a parting note into his hand, as mothers often do. She had written the words of Kierkegaard, "Purity of heart is to will one thing."

The little monk vowed to spend his life in his small cell of that monastery, getting to know his soul. But the Holy Spirit, the Great Surpriser, had another agenda.

The monastery to which he joined himself was large and famous. Early in its life it had been a monastery of the king. It had his seal and protection. All of its needs were met by the riches of the king. Even he, the king, would retreat there occasionally.

By the time the little monk came to it, centuries later, however, the monastery had relaxed most of its disciplines. It was on its own. It had been overtaken by worldliness and become a popular haven for those who only flirted with spirituality and rarely attained the real knowledge of God.

"It's easy to be religious there," neighbors reported.

And the monastery did, at least, give the little monk an opportunity to view for the first time the holy mysteries of a life totally with God.

He saw with childlike eyes what few are privileged to see. He grew in the spirit of a child, becoming an eager student in the schoolroom of holiness. Coming from prayer one day, he remarked, "I have seen things I had no right to see."

And he grew in wisdom. He learned that he did not need the greatness of a cathedral for sanctuary. He grew peaceful with himself. He grew peaceful with nature. He sometimes slept in the hollow of a giant tree. As he crouched in the dark womb of the old tree, he felt mothered by all of God's creation.

More often, though, he used the deep interior of his robe as his own little sanctuary where he could "center down" and worship God in the beauty of holiness. His robe was large, loose and tent-like. He pulled his arms into it, leaving the sleeves completely empty. He would read his Bible or prayerbook by a single slit of light that would fall between his crooked hood and the neck of his flowing robe.

For hours on end, then, in worship, study and prayer, he would be alone in this quiet chamber of wool looking for God in the darkness. Through constant mindfulness and faithful duty in the details of life, the little monk learned to confess the kingdom.

Above all else he loved the midnight prayers. While others dragged their sleepy bodies to midnight praise, he reveled in the psalms of the night, soaking in the calm and the quiet. His soul slowed down in the presence of dimmed lamps, low candles, and the clear, deep echoes that rode the coolness of the night.

"He sometimes slept in the hollow of a giant tree."

5. The Spirit of a Child

*T*he little monk grew larger and grew stronger in wisdom, yet he was physically smaller than any other adult around. The children befriended him. The little monk would join their games and play to his heart's content. Together they romped all day, until darkness made it impossible to frolic anymore. The little monk gave his all to any game. Sometimes he was leader. Sometimes he was led. His greatest joy: running freely in the children's field of dreams.

Their favorite place to play was in the big meadow by the deep river. "Let's go pick buttercups in the meadow," the little monk said to the children one bright summer day. When they got to the meadow and saw its beauty, dripping with colors, a child exclaimed, "It looks like one of my mother's watercolor paintings." Another child giggled, "What a show-off the meadow is."

The little monk smiled. " The children know," he said. "The children understand."

Their games, guided by the little monk, were played with fairness.

Shy children, who were afraid to enter the games, would often hang on for dear life to the fold of his robe, which blew softly in the breeze. The bolder children would follow his example and shelter the more timid children.

Once when a child had fallen and scraped a knee, the little monk spit into his own hand, mixed it with some loam from the earth, and added three drops of dew from a mulberry bush. He stirred it all vigorously into a dark brown salve and then, with a single swipe of his finger, rubbed it on the open wound. The hurt went away, the blood ceased to trickle and the scrape began to quickly fade.

"Nature is meant to soothe our hurts," said the little monk.

One cold, rain-drenched day another poor child set a paper boat afloat in the gutter as water rushed down the street and off to the waiting sea where the tall sails lined the blue-washed horizon. The child's ship got away from her and raced away. She cried for her lost ship. The little monk chased it in its hurried journey to the sea. The children followed. He snatched the boat just in time. "Hooray!" exclaimed the children.

But suddenly he looked up to see a runaway horse and wagon rattling toward him. As it passed by, he instinctively grabbed for the harness of the wild-eyed horse, steam snorting from its nostrils, fearful that it would charge toward the children. Too late. The wagon slammed against his hip, throwing it out of joint, and leaving the little monk breathless in his pain.

Yet, still, he bravely returned with the prodigal ship in hand to give to the child who arrived on the scene. The little monk tried to hide his limp. The young girl noticed that he was hurt, and, holding her boat for a moment, she gave it to the little monk. "I want this boat to help you feel better," she said, returning it to him. She gently held his hand and fought back the tears.

The children were learning how to comfort.

The little monk wanted no special attention. He literally tried to become invisible. Often he would find a dark corner of the monastery, wrap himself in his robe and spend a good part of days or nights contemplating the passions of Christ.

Some of the other monks, who at times searched for him throughout the monastery, had begun to call him God's turtle. Who would expect to find a man completely hidden under a ball of wool in a dim corner, lost in ecstasy, his soul celebrating the dazzling darkness?

His eyes often filled with unshed tears of gratitude. He so loved God's world. He was content to only observe. The words of Fénelon were firmly fixed in his mind: "We must learn to love personal obscurity."

Sometimes he could be found under a waiting wagon or beneath a thornbush outside of town or in a grove of sycamore trees at the edge of the great forest. His prayer would only be interrupted by moments of play with red-crested birds "trained on the finger of God," as he was fond of telling others.

From the cocoon-sized world of his loosely-woven robe the little monk would sometimes peer out with one uncovered eye in order to study the intricate pattern of a morning cobweb, the building skills of a hill of ants, the power of wild flowers in the meadow, the care with which birds fed their young, or how oak trees danced before God in the wind.

He watched the world with an open heart.

His ears, too, were open to the world. He listened to the voice of the dove, to rain battering itself into submission on cobblestone streets, to grumbling old pelicans, to summer crickets arguing with bloated bullfrogs, to babies slapping their fat knees, to mosquitoes discussing a next victim.

He listened so well that once he even heard God breathing.

The books that the little monk studied each day were the lessons of nature. His senses became unusually acute.

Animals often drank trustfully from his cupped hands.

He developed such a harmony with nature that once when a mouse scrambled under his robe and then began to ascend the little monk's leg and side, the little monk was able to remain perfectly still even while the mouse's prickly claws tickled him relentlessly. The mouse climbed by its tiny feet to one of the little monk's sleeves where lay a crumb or two of cheese left over from lunch. The mouse gobbled the cheese, squeaked a "thank you" to God, jumped behind some boxes and then ran for its life down a back alley as a wandering cat was startled by the mouse's boldness.

People often spoke of the time the little monk went into the village to beg for food or something to drink. The day had gone without success. Then he discovered a discarded wine bottle, smelling of crushed grapes. Thinking to find perhaps a few remaining drops, and knowing God would forgive his departure from his vow of abstinence, he stuck in a crooked finger only to have it lodge. Nothing he could do would loosen the finger. To break things was not in his nature, so for a week he carried the bottle on his finger beneath his robe.

Then early one morning as he slept in the meadow under the care of the stars, cold dew from heaven wetted and chilled his finger so that it popped out of the bottle like a cork. As he sucked on the wine-soaked finger, he made a brief prayer to God. He often said small prayers in admonition of the words from *The Cloud of Unknowing*, "A short prayer pierces heaven."

He became so much at home with nature that one freezing January morning, having slept in a doorway of a building, he awoke to discover he was buried by heavy snow and a crust of ice that surrounded him like an igloo. As he pushed up through his iced world, the neighborhood urchins gleefully pelted him with snowballs. "Hit him in the leg. Hit him in the stomach," they yelled. But, in the end, the little monk's own arsenal of snowballs was too much for them. The little monk was at peace. He was a joyful inhabitant of God's world.

Shortly after that, the little monk was walking down an alley when he spied something long, soft, and fluffy, hanging from a battered box. He pulled on it, only to discover that it was a furry tail with a bedraggled kitten on the other end.

The kitten was hurt, battle-scarred and limping, with a nip out of one ear looking as if it had been chomped off in some fierce fight. Patches of fur were missing from parts of its body, like a child's play-worn teddy bear. One paw was swollen with a large thorn sticking out of it. The little monk removed the thorn, kissed the paw, and rubbed it with oil.

At the back door of a tavern he was able to beg a bowl of milk. The kitten could barely lap the milk, so the little monk dipped his fingers in the milk and lifted them to the kitten's tiny mouth. She tried to mew a thanks, but no sound came out.

Even in such a broken state, you could tell that she was proud to be a cat. She knew that was God's purpose for her. She had never wanted to be anything more than an ordinary, day by day cat, man's friendly companion.

"What shall we call you?" asked the little monk out loud. "We'll call you Purr," the little monk decided.

Suddenly, he was seized by the awful knowledge of what the fall in the garden of Eden had done to even the smallest of God's innocent creatures. "Please forgive me," he said quietly to Purr. Then he whispered to all the animals of the world: "Forgive me."

Little did Purr know just how great her chosen companion and trusted friend was to become.

6. A Majestic Command

*T*he bishop came to town one day and called the entire village to worship. The bishop had many gifts, but none so compelling as his wisdom in the work of prayer. He was known far and wide as the Doctor of Prayer.

"It is time again to speak to the world," the bishop announced with an ancient voice in the great cathedral.

But he abruptly stopped in midspeech as though held by an invisible power. After a pause that seemed to last forever, he suddenly stood up from his two-hundred-year-old chair and pointed a patriarchal finger at a short, squat, barefooted monk who was all but invisible in the large congregation.

Now known to others only as "the littlest monk," he characteristically pulled himself into his robe much as a turtle disappears into its shell. His feet were covered by a robe too long, his scrawny hands folded in his lap and his hood shadowing most of his strawberry face, except for a bulbous nose that caught some shafts of sunlight pouring through the stained-glass windows of the magnificent cathedral.

Around his waist was a rope made of the braided hair from a donkey's tail.

By his side, rubbing against him, was Purr, always close, always reminding him of her presence.

As if he were about to chisel a new commandment in stone, the bishop pointed again at the little monk who still tried to hide himself.

The bishop's gaze in the little monk's direction was penetrating and relentless.

"You will be a champion of prayer," he said to the little monk in front of a surprised congregation. "Those who are fervent in prayer will always be the true heroes of the ages."

Every eye in the hushed crowd turned to the little monk. He was mortified. He had tried so hard since becoming a monk to be insignificant. "I must decrease," he often exclaimed. He had hoped that he could squeeze his little body into a ball and maybe slip from life, so that others would take no notice of him.

But now he could not hide from the bishop who motioned him forward before the people of the grand cathedral.

"A little monk shall lead them," the bishop prophesied.

"What do you want me to do?" asked the little monk cautiously.

"You will study the teachings of the great masters of prayer down throughout the centuries. You will learn the secrets of deep prayer. You will learn to pray without ceasing. You will be sent by the Spirit into the wilderness where you will be overtaken by a magnificent obsession—seeing everything through the lens of prayer. You will learn one lesson of prayer a year. One lesson a year— no more, no less," the bishop added. "The lessons are few, but involve a lifetime's work. But you will know those simple lessons so well that you can change the world."

"Why prayer?" asked the little monk.

"Prayer is the crux of the church," responded the bishop. "Jesus taught that the church, above all else, was to be a house of prayer."

"Why … why me?" the little monk stuttered. But inside he was secretly pleased. His dream of becoming a serious student of prayer had been heard.

"Because you have been chosen," answered the bishop as if that were to end the discussion.

"But why have I been chosen?" the little monk inquired, curious as to how the bishop knew his secret hope.

"I am not sure," the bishop hesitated. Then he added hastily, "Because I have decided to do so. There is no other reason. You will learn that there are some things that have nothing to do with reasons. The calling itself will transform you for the work. Simply walk in the footsteps of Abraham, your spiritual father," answered the bishop.

"But I'm not equipped for the work. I have a weak spirit," protested the little monk.

"You will soon discover, little monk, that those who give themselves to the work of prayer always have a tree full of angels in their back yard, to use William Blake's phrase," the bishop responded.

Then the bishop gave the little monk these final instructions: "You will go to the monastery of Maloo where the rugged mountains roll down to the desert. There, in that wilderness, you will be molded like clay. Where others crack, you will grow strong. Where others see only the edge of death, you will discover the fountains of life. Where others lose God, you will find him."

"Who's in charge of the monastery there?"

"The Monk who rules the world," the bishop replied.

The little monk did not understand, but still nodded as if he did.

"But how can I do this?" the little monk pleaded. "If I'm to change the world, wouldn't it be better to do it by going out into the world?"

The bishop paused, then answered. "Remember the words of Hosea, 'I will entice you into the desert and there I will speak to the depths of your heart.' I know that a monastery is the most unlikely place from which to analyze the world. On the other hand, though, there is no better place. The monastery is the true center of the world.

"You and the other disciples will be known as the Fellowship of the Desert. Go to the desert, little monk. Go to the desert. Pray without ceasing. Then one day you will have something of worth to offer the world. The church will always need at least one strong friend of prayer."

"I'll probably have to have a map to Maloo, won't I?" inquired the little monk.

"Yes, you'll need a map," answered the bishop, handing him a worn, tattered map, folded tightly.

The little monk was eager to unfold the map.

"No," said the bishop. "Later, when you're at the coast and ready to board ship."

One last thing was on the little monk's mind. "May I take my cat? Her name is Purr. She would be lost without me."

The bishop frowned. His demeanor grew stern. No worthy monk should have any worldly attachment, thought the bishop.

"Animals praise God, too, in their own way, don't they?" asked the little monk.

This interesting possibility struck the bishop's sense of humor. The bishop smiled. "I commission you both, then, to become captains of prayer."

With that, the bishop dismissed the little monk.

The little monk slowly turned to take the long walk to the massive doors of the glorious cathedral. Halfway to the doors, a child reached out, touched him, and pushed a slingshot into his hand, a weapon with which to do battle against the forces of evil.

Every eye followed him as he trod the path alone to the

outside of the cathedral and into the daylight. With each step he pulled himself more and more into the inner sanctum of his robe. His baggy robe hung to the ground. A small cloud of dust billowed up behind him, caused by his sagging robe dragging the ground.

7. Prayer from the Deepest Well

O nce outside, he stopped at the village well to pray for his journey. He was confused and bewildered. The well was one of his favorite praying places. "Hello," he shouted into the well. Hollow echoes helloed him back. His mother had used the well first as her own praying place, and then, when the little monk was yet a boy, his mother brought him to the center of town and to the well. "Remember," she often told him, "always pray from the deepest well."

Now he peered down into the still waters of the old well. He dropped a stone into the well, heard a splash and watched the water settle again. He leaned far over the well and stared into its depths. Long ago he had written a poem about the well:

Is it by accident, design or will,
    That I fall headlong into the deepest well,
Where dark murky waters o'er me steal?
    And nothing 'round seems firm or real,
Except the growing fear within my soul.
    At first I fight the strong pull
Of the deepest well, then go numb,
    At last surrendering to whatever may come,
Heaven or hell.
    Waiting, in the silence, the long silence—alone,

"Prayer from the Deepest Well"

I float to the bottom of the well, soft and slow
　　Where a thousand endless rivers flow,
From God's eternal throne.

He also remembered what the oldtimers used to say. They said that if you stood in the deepest part of a dark well you could see the farthest stars of heaven even at mid-day.

"Father, I want to see the stars," he said. Nothing came back except the echo of his own voice—"STARS, Stars, starrrs."

But now it was time to journey.

The little monk left the village at a turtle's pace and hobbled toward the horizon, with all of his destiny in the hands of God. "Obedience always begins with a first step," his mother had often told him. His faithful companion, Purr, plodded beside him, trusting and secure and ready to follow wherever her master led.

8. The Journey Toward God

*T*he little monk followed the narrow path from the village that led across the high bridge into the gateway of the dense forest. He plunged through a giant thickness of trees, and came to a clearing in the woods. He was awestruck with the golden light from the harvest moon. "God provides," he realized. He ate a sparse dinner late at night, and then lay on his back in weariness with Purr beside him. He surveyed the sky for some small token that God was still there.

It took him several grueling weeks to get to the seacoast where he was to take ship before winter set in. Winter is not the season for long journeys.

Before boarding ship, he took out the map that the bishop had given him. It was so brittle that it broke apart in his hands. He laid the pieces on the ground and fit them together like a puzzle. He found his own position on the map, as well as positions of other towns and countries. Then he noticed a strange thing. Various places on the map were marked with these words, "This may be Maloo."

Such a turn of events saddened him. How would he ever find the real Maloo?

"Remember, your exodus is only a journey toward God," the bishop had said.

Trusting the bishop's wisdom, the little monk boarded the waiting ship. "O Great Jehovah, through cloud and fiery pillar guide me onward in my journey," he prayed to the Shepherd of the Seas.

"Where are you going?" asked the captain.

"To Maloo," answered the little monk.

"And where might that be?" the captain asked. "I've been all over the world and I've never heard of Maloo."

"Maloo is a special place. Few people have ever found it," said the little monk, hoping he would not be questioned more about it, since he really didn't know where it was himself.

"Which way is Maloo?" the captain continued to press.

The little monk turned full circle three times and with fake assurance pointed in the direction that the ship was already headed. "That's the way to Maloo," he announced with all the confidence he could muster. To Purr, though, he whispered quietly, "I hope I know Maloo when I find it."

The trip across the sea was uneventful until, late one night, a gusty storm set in, like an eighth day of creation. The little monk awoke to the sickening bounce of the boat as wave after wave crashed against the deck, rocking the boat like a hammock. He reached down on his stomach to where Purr usually slept. He wanted to calm her. Storms and darkness and shadows frightened her.

Purr was gone. The little monk bolted out of bed. He couldn't find her. She was not under the bunk, nor below the table, nor up in the window.

"Have you seen my cat?" he asked of everyone as he fought the winds to search every corner of the ship. "Probably washed overboard and halfway to France by now," one of the sailors said matter-of-factly. The little monk bowed his head and prayed, "Father of oceans and storms, please take care of Purr. She needs me so very much. She's a weak cat and has many fears. She's very frightened by the phantoms of the sea. Amen."

"That's the way to Maloo,"
he announced, with all the confidence he could muster.

The dejected little monk started for his room. Then he heard it, riding on the wind—a tiny "mew." "That's Purr," he shouted, heading for the bow of the ship. There, nestled in the arms of a sea nymph figurehead, was Purr, wet and wild, but still all intact. "I'll get her," one of the sailors yelled as he took a fish net to scoop her off the sea nymph and pull her back on board.

The little monk grabbed her and nuzzled his cheek against hers. "I love you, Purr," he said, putting his nose against hers. "You are a brave cat."

Over the next several days he watched Purr to see how she had really fared as a result of the storm. Sitting on deck one day, he wrote in his journal: "It seems that Purr is still afraid of the storms. Last night dark rain clouds formed again. Purr hissed at them until she finally wore herself to sleep."

"What are you writing?" another passenger asked.

"A journal."

"What's that?" asked the passenger.

"When one goes on a journey, one should keep a journal of what happens," replied the little monk. "Journey and journal are two words that have the same father."

"Well, then, perhaps I should keep a journal. I'm on a journey, too," the passenger said.

"We're all on a journey, a journey inward to the edge of glory and light," the little monk responded.

By morning the ship had landed on the coast of France. The search for Maloo began in earnest. The little monk visited cathedrals and monasteries and religious sites throughout the land, but no one had heard of a place called Maloo. He loved France and its special kind of spirituality—so orderly, so delicate, like fine lace. He hoped that he would discover Maloo there. His doubts told him to go on. Still, he lingered there longer than he should have. Finally he moved across the mountains to Italy.

His pilgrimage through legendary towns brought him at last to the Eternal City, Rome itself. The strange mixture of heaven and earth that was Rome captured his imagination unlike anything else. Trudging around the city for several days in a spiritual stupor, he finally said to his cat, "Purr, this has to be Maloo. The bishop must have been using Maloo as a code name. We'll settle here."

There were any number of religious communities to join. He was welcomed with open arms. Over the next several months, the little monk reveled in the spiritual banquet set before him in Rome. He needed nothing else. The glories of Rome had kidnaped his heart. Every new encounter with the earthy holiness of the city persuaded him even more that this was, in fact, Maloo.

Then, one day, in the Sistine Chapel, he marveled aloud at the ceilings. "Magnificent," his voice echoed. He stopped in his tracks, for the echo reminded him of something from long ago—a forgotten well. His mother's words came back to him: "Always pray from the deepest well."

The weight of glory that was Rome filled his soul abundantly. Why then was his mind starting to play tricks on him? What was this growing uneasiness that maybe he had not found Maloo after all? Could Maloo offer anything more than Rome?

Not long after, though, he left Rome for Athens. In Athens he discovered another kind of temptation. Where Rome had captured his heart, Athens stole his mind and imagination. The sculptures, the paintings, the exquisite buildings stirred his love of the arts as nothing else had. He walked where great philosophers had trod. Here was the fountain of wisdom and the great ideas that had changed the world.

How could he not take advantage of such stirring of the mind and spirit? he wondered. "Now everything is starting to fall into place, Purr," he said as they stood before some ancient vases in a museum. "This is why God led me early on to be a potter. My calling is to be a godly artist, mixing clay with the mysteries of the kingdom. In a different way this could be the Maloo that I'm seeking." There was a tremendous sense of peace for him in that notion. Surely God would not give me a passion for art without cause, he thought.

Several months later, on a hot summer day, the little monk worked away in an outdoor studio. Purr was asleep in a large unfinished bowl. The damp clay was a cool place to nap. As the little monk finished a delicate vase and held it up to the light, the light blinded him for a moment. His eyes watered, then cleared to a brilliant focus. He thought about that instant of blindness and wondered what else he might be blind to. His heart was held hostage to the wisdom of the world. Athens has made me whole in a way, he thought, but it's not Maloo.

He knew that in forsaking Athens he would leave behind a part of him that would make him feel incomplete, perhaps forever. The call to Maloo, however, continued to haunt him.

A week later he and Purr journeyed to the east in search of Maloo once again. He sailed for Turkey with all intents of then heading south toward Jerusalem. Something prevented him from going in that direction, though. He had a strong urging to continue on straight to the Caspian Sea. "This has got to be wrong," he thought. "How can I pass by the land where my Lord lived and died?" Yet somehow he knew that Jerusalem was for another time. He needed to learn more, much more, before walking in the footsteps of his Lord.

9. The Fellowship of Faith

"**Y**our exodus is only a journey toward God," said the little monk over and over.

The only one who heard him was Purr. The little monk was becoming lonely and discouraged.

One hot day, wearied and thirsty, he stopped by a village of the Orthodox faith. Sitting near the well, he was approached by the leader of the village who welcomed him and invited him to stay for a while.

The little monk was hungry for some words of faith. And, over the weeks that he remained there, he learned a great deal from the villagers. He learned especially about practicing the presence of Christ. "St. Symeon the New Theologian said that we should constantly feel the presence of God as a pregnant woman feels the presence of the babe in her womb," he was told. He remembered that image whenever he saw a pregnant woman, her own life intricately entwined with the child growing within.

"Let us teach you how to pray without ceasing by using the Jesus Prayer," they said. "What's that?" asked the little monk.

The Jesus Prayer, as he learned, was very simple: "Lord Jesus Christ, Son of God, be merciful to me a sinner." That's certainly the gospel in a nutshell, he thought. "How do I use it?" he asked. "Say it over and over until it forms a rhythm with your breathing and your heartbeat," they answered. "Such on-going prayer keeps the soul in a perpetual presence before God, even though one's outer life may be busy and filled with work and daily duties."

His time in this Orthodox community was valuable in helping to shape his inner landscape. He filled his journal with fresh insights and his heart with many treasures. The time had come, though, for the little monk to move on.

He took out the map that the bishop had given him. He wanted to study it again. Maybe he had missed some clue. He laid the pieces of the map on the ground by the side of the road. He examined the map in detail. He had traveled already to the end of the bishop's map. None of the places he had visited were Maloo. The little monk would have to go on by faith.

Then he remembered something that the bishop had said. "Maloo is always just beyond where you think it is."

He tried to reason what that could mean. An idea, though, came to him. He would take the bishop's map to a local map maker to see what he might think of it.

"Do you suppose you can help me find Maloo?" asked the little monk. "A mountain might be near it," he added.

"Never heard of it," said the map maker, looking as if he had lived too long on the open seas and fought too many sharks. "Here's something interesting, though. All those places that might have been Maloo seem, roughly, to form a fairly straight line, like stepping-stones or stations on the way to Mount Maloo. If I were you, I would keep on going in that line and sail the Caspian. If this is the right map, Maloo has to be that way."

The little monk wondered about the wisdom of the strange map maker. Perhaps the sea has weathered his mind too much, the little monk thought. But with no other sense of direction to go on, he continued the journey to the Caspian Sea.

Although the season was changing, the Caspian Sea was still furious and evil that time of year. The ship was

The little monk studies the map to Maloo.

soon blown off course, and they were shipwrecked at the southern end of the Caspian. The captain shouted from the ship's bow which was stuck on a reef, "We're ship-wrecked. The journey's over. Abandon ship."

Purr and the little monk swam ashore, fighting the waves and the undercurrents, terribly frightened and tired. On shore they looked back for the broken ship that had slammed against the reef. The ship had already slipped beneath the waters.

They were several miles from town. They trudged in exhaustion along the meandering path, the little monk's head drooped on his chest, his eyes toward the ground and his mind wandering. Suddenly Purr mewed loudly. "Ouch," the little monk yelled as he brushed against a bramblebush, his leg torn open by the thorns. He stooped to nurse his leg. He pulled a sharp thorn from his leg, started to throw it away, but then kept it as a reminder. Purr licked his leg protectively.

When the little monk finally stood up, he looked on the fields before him. How peculiar! he thought. This land looks familiar, yet I know I've never been here before. He smelled the air and rubbed a handful of soil between his fingers. This is a good land, he said to himself.

In the distance was a sower casting seed from a full bag. He went over to him. "Do you happen to know the way to Maloo?" he asked the sower.

The sower stopped his sowing, wiped his sweated brow, and set his heavy bag on the ground. He paused, pulled some chaff out of a handful of seed, and then let it run through his fingers. He pointed vaguely toward the south, to the province beyond the river.

"Are you sure you want to go to Maloo?" asked the sower, looking over his intruder.

"Yes, I have been sent there by my bishop," the little

monk explained. "Can you tell me about Maloo?" the little
monk continued.

"Maloo?" A long pause. "It's a place of windy nights
and sturdy days. It's a land as old as pomegranates and
mustard seeds, yet as new as a patch of lilies on a spring
day. It's a spacious land, with acres of grace. But most of
all, Maloo is a very thin place."

The little monk thought he meant small and asked
about it.

"No, not small. Thin. The distance there between heav-
en and earth, between God and his people, is no more
than the thickness of a curtain around one's bed at night.
The saints have built such a ladder of prayer in Maloo that
angels ascend and descend on the place. The hosts of
heaven seem to cavort there with the likes of ordinary
men. Maloo is so thin one can see the face of God."

The little monk was awed by what the sower said. He
remembered that when Jesus died the veil of the temple
was torn in two so that common people found themselves
staring with astonishment into the Holy of Holies, the last
thing they expected to see. That, too, was a very thin
place.

"Once you've been to Maloo, you'll never be the same.
God has a cottage there, you know," the sower said curiously and returned to casting seed over the land.

The little monk climbed a high mountain and followed
well-worn trails that laced through peaks and valleys until
the world seemed to end abruptly at the edge of the
ancient desert sands. Far above, on the steep cliffs, was the
magnificent presence of Maloo, almost dream-like in the
morning haze.

The monastery itself lay to the east, perched high on a
ledge halfway up the most majestic of mountains. From
this precipice where the monastery sat, one could see the
crowns of a thousand hills, and yet still view the eternal

sands of the desert that lay quietly and peacefully in the distance.

In silence, the little monk carried all of his worldly belongings in a sack made from a scrap of sail taken from the now sunken ship. He struggled on toward the monastery. Loyal Purr tagged along. Suddenly they both stopped. Together they gazed in wonder.

The brilliant colors of the morning sky presented their glorious rainbows before them. The forest offered a thousand spices and fragrances as its gift to them. Rabbits, squirrels, and owls spoke quietly and sincerely. Mountain brooks babbled a gentle song. A nearby waterfall offered fresh renewal in foam and mist. Sunbeams blinked and darted about. Sheep, with their newborn lambs, frolicked in the open fields.

The brilliance of the scene moved something very deep within the little monk. He loved nature so much; he always had, even as a young lad. How he wished—still—that he could hold all of nature in his pocket.

"Finally, I've come home," breathed the little monk.

He sealed his awe of Maloo with this prayer from the Psalms: "May there be abundance of peace here until the moon shall be no more."

10. Lessons from the Task

*T*he little monk arrived at the old gate which swung on heavy bronze hinges. He had to knock for a long time. It seemed at first that no one was there. But finally a weather-crusted bolt slid roughly in its slot like some ancient rifle being cocked for shooting. A tall, lanky, bearded monk, lost in meditation, greeted him wordlessly, and then gestured for the little monk to follow him.

In silence the little monk followed the brother who mumbled a prayer to himself in rhythm to their walk. Purr's brown eyes were alert and ready to inspect this new world.

The little monk arrived at his barren cell. Purr quickly scampered under the bed. By the time the little monk had put away his things, another monk entered with a basin of water and a towel. He knelt before the little monk and silently washed the little monk's feet. He dried them, and, to the little monk's chagrin, kissed his feet. Purr's brown eyes peered out curiously from under the bed.

Then the little monk was taken to the chapel where psalms were being chanted and the word of God read aloud. The power and glory of the words echoed in his ears. Then silence reigned throughout the chapel, except for low murmurs of prayer. He found endless healing in this sacramental silence. The little monk took out his journal and wrote: "Silence empties us so that we can be filled with God."

Every stone and statue, every brick walkway and bar-

ren room of the tranquil monastery was soaked by centuries of prayer.

The diversity of the community at Maloo amazed the
little monk. It seemed that all branches of the Christian
church were represented here, believers from every kingdom and tribe and nation and wing of the visible church.

The monastery at Maloo was a melting pot of the various beliefs and traditions. "This is an experiment in uni-
versal Christian community where both the riches and the
oddities of practices of believers worldwide are respect-
ed," one of the brothers told him. "That is what Maloo is
all about."

At first the little monk was given no work to do. "You
are to have several weeks of sabbath, a time to tarry in the
Lord's leisure," one of the brothers informed him.

He often spent part of each day at the well, sipping the
cold water and peering into the depths of the ivy and
moss-covered well, listening for echoes that might fill him
again with memories of home.

The little monk carried a copy of St. Francis' "Canticle
of the Sun" clipped securely in his journal. He took it out
often and read it aloud for all creation to hear, especially
these words:

> Praised be my Lord God for all his
> creatures, especially for our brother
> the sun, who brings us the day and
> who brings us the light....
>
> Praised be my Lord for our sister the moon,
> and for the stars, which he has set
> clear and lovely in heaven.
>
> Praised be my Lord for our brother
> the wind, and for the air and clouds,

calms and all weather by which you
uphold life in all creatures.

He was relaxed and content in this holy land.

One sun-bleached morning when the little monk started off for a day in the forest, he was informed by one of the brothers that he, the little monk, was to go to work that day.

"What am I to do?" he asked eagerly.

"You will be the stone-bearer," answered the brother.

"But isn't that the hardest task of all?" wondered the little monk.

After a heavy rain, the bruised riverbed would dry up, leaving large rocks and stones, naked in the sun.

These stones were then carried by the monks, one at a time, three miles away to the monastery which looked almost ghostly-Gothic under the shadow of the lofty mountain. The stones and rocks were used for various purposes from foundations to fireplaces.

On his first trip down to the riverbed, he felt relieved to see another monk there to help. It was the same monk who had washed his feet on the day he arrived at the monastery of Maloo. They worked in silence. The little monk was completely exhausted at the end of the day. He dropped on his bed, like a sack of salt tossed in the back of a waiting wagon, and slept through dinner. They awakened him in time for Vespers, but he was so weary he could not pray. His mind fought the very thought of praying.

Dreary days crawled like snails into weary weeks. The work was relentless. The stones were heavy and soon the little monk found his body bending itself in an oval shape around the stones. He was pulled into a ball of misshapen flesh—back bent over, shoulders stooped, arms rounded, and belly pushed in.

"He was relieved to see another monk there to help."

His partner, however, seemed more strengthened each day by the work as if he were living off some secret food and drink. "The bread of angels," the other monks called it.

One day as the little monk lifted a heavy stone it fell to the ground and broke apart. He left it there, knowing that the next storm would cover it again as if it had never been. He began to dig out another rock which was half-buried in the thick mud. He was startled to hear the brother speak. It ruptured the long silence between them: "Broken stones are more valuable than all the rest. They're more usable."

That night, though, he made a decision. He would go to the leader of the monastery—Servant Jonathan, a brother whom, he just realized, he had never seen since coming to the monastery. He would tell the leader that he just didn't have the strength to continue such difficult work day on end.

After the solitude of his cell and a difficult time of prayer at Evensong, the little monk slipped through a crayon-black midnight to knock at Servant Jonathan's door. After a short wait, a gentle voice invited him in.

"Come, little monk, have some soup, cake and goat cheese," the voice said in tones that rolled through the room with the warmth of a long lost friend.

He entered a plain, austere room, lighted only by a flickering candle piercing the darkness. When the little monk arrived at the offered chair, he stopped abruptly. He recognized the leader. The leader was someone he had seen before. He was the one who had washed his feet, the one who carried stones with him.

"How—how long have you been the leader here?" stammered the little monk as he dropped into the chair.

"Since I came here twenty years ago," replied the leader.

"But why? Why the washing of feet? The carrying of stones?" inquired the little monk.

"Because I am among you as one who serves," replied the leader, placing a worn, calloused hand kindly on the little monk's shaved head.

When the little monk could put it all together, he realized that this man was the living example of what it means to be a servant leader, to serve as Jesus did.

"Little monk, be anxious for nothing. Accept the work given to you as if it were the most important work in the kingdom of God. Find Christ in the stones. He's there, you know. Oh, not literally, but metaphorically. When you carry these stones, you bear the body of Christ," said the leader.

The little monk pondered this. "I was so exhausted and weary," remarked the little monk. "I thought I was being punished, having to carry all that heavy rock."

"His yoke is easy and his burden is light. The work of God should always send us forth as roaring lions," Jonathan told him, offering him some soup and a corner of cinnamon cake.

The two talked far into the night—a time of great learning for the little monk. As he stood to leave, Jonathan instructed, "Remember what the Desert Fathers taught, 'Go and sit in your cell. Your cell will teach you all things.'"

The little monk became an expert in the uses of stone. From some of the stones he fashioned prayer huts built on ageless rock, from others he chipped the gravel for paths worn away by the feet of monks marching seven times a day to prayer.

He committed his learning to the pages of his journal.

In the following years, the little monk served diligently as the stone-bearer. He learned the hard lessons of discipleship.

At low points in his life, the wind would carry to him the sweet incense of mountain flowers, the fierce rains would scrub him clean, the forest animals would call his name far into the night and he would often read magical messages in the worn pebbles of the shallow streams.

But still, the work took its toll. The little monk went through the motions of his duties with little expectation of anything ever changing much. Servant Jonathan noticed that the little monk had been overtaken by "the dark night of the soul," and that his inner well had gone dry.

The work was so long, so endless, so constant that, to the little monk, there seemed to be little room left for joy. "Sometimes I feel as though I have to borrow from tomorrow's grace in order to bear today's burdens," the little monk sighed to Servant Jonathan.

Jonathan reminded him of the words of the Lord to Angela of Foligno: "I have not loved you in jest; my love for you is no trifling thing."

For the little monk, struggling along a day at a time in the cold, lonely monastery, hidden under the shadow of the high mountain, time moved as slowly as a sleepless night.

11. Our Daily Bread

*O*ne day the little monk's life changed dramatically. Servant Jonathan assigned him a new job.

"You will make our daily bread," he said.

"I'm to make bread?" asked the surprised little monk.

"You'll be our baker. From now on you'll work in the kitchen," Jonathan said.

The little monk's first attempts at baking bread were awful failures. Wednesday's loaves were as hard as rocks. Friday's bread was too heavy and underbaked. Saturday's bread was badly burned.

The little monk sat down on top of an overturned lard bucket, holding a loaf of the ruined bread. Tears formed in the corners of his eyes and rolled down his cheeks.

Servant Jonathan came by to see how he was doing. "Weep not for yesterday's bread," he advised.

"I'm such a failure," said the little monk.

"Learn the lessons of the bread," Jonathan advised.

The little monk looked at the bread doubtfully. How can I study bread? he thought to himself as Jonathan left.

He took a loaf of bread and turned it in his hands. He squinted his eyes. Squinting, he had discovered, helps inner vision. But the bread yielded no secrets. In despair, he cried, "I'm an undone man." He broke the loaf in half to see if there might be a story told there, but the secret of the bread was closed as tightly as a book with a lock and a key.

Suddenly the air felt so heavy and stifling that it seemed

"The little monk sat down on top of an overturned lard bucket, holding a loaf of the ruined bread."

to magnify the clanging of the pots and pans into a deafening roar. The little monk held his ears, desperately hoping for some quiet to calm his raw nerves. When the bread was finally ready for the day, he took leave of his helpers and went to the chapel seeking a quiet holy hour before Communion.

Kneeling at the altar rail, waiting for Communion, he said his prayers and meditated about the growing darkness and void in his heart. "O God, I have such little passion left," he confessed.

Purr tagged along behind him and now lay in a quiet furry ball next to him. She licked his hand. He reached down to stroke her head and rub her ears. Her rough, wet tongue tickled his hand. He smiled. Innocent love is so freely given, thought the little monk. Her only desire in all the world was to be with him. He could hear the soft purring of his contented companion as she lay next to him.

The priest passed by to serve him Communion. "The body of Christ, little monk, the body of Christ broken for you," the priest declared. The little monk crossed himself rather mechanically and opened his mouth to receive the waiting bread. What on earth is the secret of this bread? he asked himself. Then like echoes from a deep well, long-forgotten words about Christ from one of the saints, Julian of Norwich, rang like clear bells in the little monk's ears: "Love is his meaning."

In that holy moment when his tongue touched the silent bread, and love surged through him, he knew for certain the secret of the bread.

He picked up Purr and rocked her in his arms, just as God had done with him.

"The secret," he later confided to Servant Jonathan, "the secret is to rest contentedly and leisurely in the love of God, the one who made us for himself. The bread praises its maker by resting silently in its own being."

"Yes, and like clay pots, we, too, were made for holding something—the love of God. Nothing else matters than to be what we were made to be—containers of love," Servant Jonathan added.

Although his bread that day turned out no better than previous times, the little monk served it at dinner that evening with great pleasure, knowing well the lesson the bread had taught him.

He also did not fail to notice, with a slight smile, the other monks who graciously struggled to swallow the heavy, undone bread of the day. "Manna from rocks," one brother called it jokingly.

The little monk committed this learning, too, to the pages of his journal.

12. The Beauty of the Silence

"*T*he potter is dead," Servant Jonathan announced sadly. "You will now be our potter," he informed the little monk.

This confused him, for his background as a potter seemed to make the new job too easy. Later that day, he went to see Servant Jonathan. He was willing to submit to the leader's assignment, but felt he needed to discuss the situation with his spiritual director.

"Just as you were mistaken in thinking your last task was too hard, you are mistaken in thinking this one is too easy," the leader challenged. "Call not that hard which the Spirit can make easy and call not that easy by which the Spirit wishes to teach hard lessons."

Weeks and months piled up into years, like worn rocks in a dry riverbed. The little monk learned new secrets of wisdom in clay pots. He learned the various stresses and weaknesses of the vessels of clay, as well as the infinite ways in which they could be molded or strengthened.

He became a master in seeing cracks hidden from the eyes of others. Some pots gave every evidence of being a work of art. But the little monk, sometimes just by lifting the pot, could tell its hidden weakness. Plain pots that some might overlook for lack of beauty, the little monk would often show to be the strongest and most useful of all.

"A person is much like a clay pot," the leader told the little monk one day. From then on the little monk trans-

"A host of people came to the little monk for counsel and advice."

ferred his wisdom of clay pots to the variety of people he met in the flow of village and monastery life.

A host of people came to the little monk for counsel and advice. He found himself talking endlessly through busy days, while also wishing more and more for the beauty of the silence that had left him. He was torn between speaking in order to help others and seeking solitude in order to help himself.

Servant Jonathan saw this dilemma. With the right touch of reasoned compassion, he told the little monk, "Let me give you some practical words to restore your balance."

"If you talk too much to your wearied clay pots you will never fully understand all of their characteristics. Fine clay pots are molded in silence. So it is with people. You do not always shape people by words, but sometimes with the simple message of silence," the leader exclaimed.

So it was that through the slow ebb of time, the little monk learned all the more what he did not know about clay pots or common people.

The little monk took in the hard-earned truths of patience, silence and solitude, virtues that lead one, at last, to the house of the Holy Spirit.

And so these truths were also committed to the pages of his journal to be read and read again in times of doubt and times of trouble.

Like all of the ancient seekers, he, too, was a master climber of the ladder of holy secrets.

13. The Fourth Counselor

*T*he little monk's journal was becoming a valuable record of a soul tamed by God.

He had started this lifetime of journaling as a very young monk. Now, as the years passed, the key spiritual disciplines of patience, silence and solitude, and many valuable virtues had been lived and learned and recorded in the journal of the little monk.

These are the lessons that make us feel at home, part of the family, at one in the fellowship of the Holy Spirit.

The simple truths that were recorded into the little monk's Bible—his journal—revealed the tell-tale signs of how God sometimes winks at us. It showed us how often God allows us a peek at the mysteries of his kingdom, much like a magician who lets us see how one trick is done in order to entice with a better one.

The words that inspired the birth of this journal were the words of Jesus after the feeding of the five thousand. The little monk thought of this lesson daily:

According to the Scriptures, when all of the hungry crowds were well-fed, Jesus did not leave it at that. Jesus told his disciples to pick up the leftovers. "Let nothing be wasted," were the inspirational words of Jesus.

These words made a lasting impression on the little monk who decided then and there to "save" the pieces of his life—insights, memories, and happenings—in the pages of a home-made book, created by putting some paper together and then sewing leather covers on the front and back for protection. Thus was the creation of his journal—his most precious of all possessions.

He called this journal his "fourth counselor."

"What do you mean by fourth counselor?" someone once asked.

"We all have a number of counselors available to us. Three of these counselors we know well: the church, our friends, and prayer. The journal is our fourth counselor. In the silence and solitude of my journal I often counsel myself, and wrestle with the issues of my life," the little monk responded.

"But more," he continued, "the journal is a time machine. It allows me to move back and forth between the past, the future and the present, to hold time out in front of me like a globe that can be spun round and round. That way I can make important adjustments in the hurts of the past, the fears of the future and the uncertainties of the present."

As he became more committed to the truths placed in his journal, so too did the little monk become dedicated in his search for truth.

He would often spend time high up in the lonely mountains where the three winds blow. The little monk willed one thing with all his heart. "Let me be reshaped by silence and solitude," he prayed.

He knew that Jesus himself often slipped away to "a lonely place apart" to be "alone." The little monk was proud to share this experience with Christ. "Alone with the Alone," the Church Fathers used to say.

Being "Alone with the Alone" had nothing to do with loneliness, he learned. "Solitude is of the spirit; loneliness is of the flesh," he printed deliberately in his journal.

"He would often spend time high up in the lonely mountains where the winds blow."

"The kingdom of God is within you," Jesus had said. The little monk wrote these words, too, in his journal, as well as the words of Teresa of Avila: "Settle yourself in solitude and you will come upon him in yourself."

A leader had once told the little monk, "The trouble with the world is that there is not enough silence."

When the little monk was away from his journal, albeit not very often, he would make a habit of writing messages in the earth. "It is good for God's other creation, the earth, to receive the word of truth, too."

And the little monk smiled at yet another truth uncovered.

"Remember that thou art dust and to dust thou shalt return." These words also came to the little monk. To know that we are only dust caused him to shudder suddenly, until one overwhelming thought grabbed him: "Our only hope is this—our Savior, like us, was a man of dust, a sleeper in the ground, wrapped in linen, myrrh and ashes, eager to rise again from the tyrant dust, his soul starved for the glory that he had left behind with the Father."

How wonderful to grow in peace. How wonderful to grow in tranquility, realized the little monk. My restless soul is becoming calm, he concluded.

Then he wrote in the sands: "Silence is freedom. Solitude liberates us completely." A companion monk on a desert journey had once quoted to him a line about silence from St. John of the Cross: "My house being now all stilled ..."

The companion added: "If you've ever entered a house when no one else was home, you know the utter peace that reigns there undisturbed."

And these words, too, were committed to the pages of his journal.

14. The Seeds of Leadership

Several years later, the little monk's training in solitude climaxed in his appointment to a new and different task: Keeper of the Seeds.

From the various trees, plants, herbs, and flowers he was to gather, sort, and preserve fruitful seeds.

The study of the life and growth of seeds fired new passion in the little monk.

Words from the Scriptures about "holy seed," "incorruptible seed," and "good seed" gave him much upon which to meditate.

"Every soul is like a grain of mustard seed," Servant Jonathan said one day. The little monk put that together with the words of Jesus, "Except a grain of wheat fall into the ground and die, it cannot bring forth life."

One day when working in the undergrowth of the forest, the little monk was seeking some lost seeds which had fallen. As he searched through the forest, he accidentally stepped on the seeds, crushing them deep into the fallen pine needles and rotted leaves. He was stunned at his carelessness. Then he realized: however careless he had been, even crushed seeds will grow when nurtured by God-given gifts of rain and sun and wind. What mysteries there are in the stories of innocent seeds. He cried aloud in the forest, "Holy, holy, holy is the Lord God of pine cones and hazelnuts."

"The seed is the word of God," he wrote passionately in his journal.

"...he was to gather, sort and preserve fruitful seeds."

The little monk loved his work with seeds. No matter the time of day or night, he always carried some seeds with him as a token of his devotion. He kept three special seeds in his pocket to remind him of the three great virtues: faith, hope and love. When a brother died—one who was the Keeper of the Seeds before him—they placed this on his tombstone: "In memory of the seeds, I now become one with them in the deep soil of the universe."

"I could spend a lifetime teaching the lessons of the seeds," the little monk said. "How I might make a difference in the world if only I could show others how a person is like a seed—a seed that lies dormant for years, ready to burst into life at the first word from God," the little monk said to a group who had gathered to hear him speak.

"A leader is one who listens," Brother Jonathan told the little monk firmly. "A leader is one who nurtures growth."

The little monk realized that Brother Jonathan was once again turning to the subject of leadership as he had done quite often in their recent discussions. Yet the little monk did not feel quite worthy of leadership, and so he remained silent in the face of such awesome challenge and responsibility.

Brother Jonathan, determined to open the little monk to new possibilities for the Spirit to work in his life, continued to impress upon the little monk his own hard-earned truths. "Compassion and common sense are often the first casualties of new leadership." "Remember these words, little monk," he said.

"Listen to the inner voice of leadership," continued Jonathan. "Observe how troubled many leaders are today. They think their problems are with delegating, problem solving, and managing time, but these are only symptoms. The real problems are problems of trust, of love, and of empowerment. Without trust the whole world wearies.

Without love, all relationships rust away. Without empowerment, people abandon their dreams."

"Listen to the inner voice of leadership, little monk," said Jonathan again. "Lead with your heart. You cannot force anything around you to grow simply by casting out seeds of wisdom. New growth must be nurtured, protected, cared for and faced toward God's sun. So is the responsibility of leadership—you must first nurture, then protect, then offer care, and finally face your trusts toward the Son of God. We all know this truth down deep inside of us, at the root of our being. We already have all we really need in order to lead. Too often, though, we suppress that and go by worldly standards or by exercising cold, calculating power. Don't count on the world to teach you leadership. Its goals are bankrupt. Listen to your heart. Listen to the inner voice of leadership."

Brother Jonathan took the little monk to the window. "When you understand the meaning of why that speckled hen pecking corn over there by the barn exists, you will be a true leader," Brother Jonathan said.

The little monk squinted to see the hen more clearly but still struggled to understand what a hen would have to do with leadership.

Yet the little monk still gave all of himself completely and totally to the simple jobs that were his at the monastery at Maloo. These few tasks done well, he thought, would eventually fit him for a genuine place in the fellowship of Maloo.

But tasks done well do not create a leader, sighed Jonathan to himself. I must allow the little monk to grow in his own time, in his own way, molded personally by the gentle hands of God.

One evening the brothers discovered that the little monk had not returned from the seed shed. They went to look for him. They found him unconscious, lying on the dirt floor, still clutching a fistful of seeds. His foot was twisted severely. His hip was a swollen hump.

"Is he dead?" a brother gasped.

"I don't know," Servant Jonathan answered. He thought his own heart would break.

15. The Divine Wounding

"**I**s he going to live?" Sister Anne asked.

"I don't know," replied the leader. "We'll have to let God tell us that."

"What's wrong with him?" Sister Anne asked.

"His hip is swollen and infected. Gangrene might be setting in," the leader cautioned.

Sister Anne wiped the little monk's brow with cool water from the mineral springs. The little monk did not stir. Instead, he fell deeper into the dark cave of the mind, where the soul waits for a signal, the flutter of an angel's wings, to know whether to go back or to go on.

Sister Anne and Servant Jonathan stood, breathed a silent prayer and left, closing the door behind them.

In that endless timelessness known only to those who walk the valley of the shadow of death, the little monk's thoughts became a river of fiery love seeking to spill itself into the ocean of God's presence.

Some creature from the dark corner of the mind leaped upon the little monk. It seemed to be part man, part bird, part angel—a seraphim perhaps. The creature wrestled the little monk to the ground. They were face to face, rolling on the ground. The creature's breath was the breath of fire and brimstone, yet mixed with some sweet fragrance like incense from the altar. The little monk was almost suffocating in the feathered wings of the creature.

Then it touched his side with unspeakable power. Finally, with one sharp claw, it slashed at the little monk's

*"Some creature from the dark corner of the mind
leaped upon the little monk."*

forehead. Blood flowed freely down a face as gaunt and drawn as a starving orphan. The little monk reached up to feel a gash, a sacred scar, to be carried forever. Suddenly the little monk's soul was burned again and again by hot cinders of holiness falling from the altar of God.

In the time that it takes an angel to blink, the little monk landed back in life as a door closed and a cold wind rushed through the window and across his bed. The little monk awoke with a chill.

He could barely lift his eyelids. When he did they fell closed again right away. He struggled for quite some time to get his eyes fixed open. Focusing was hard. Everything swirled, contracted and expanded in a blur that folded in upon itself.

"Little monk ... little monk," the leader called.

Finally, the little monk could see, but still as if in a dream.

"You seemed as if you were having a nightmare of sorts," Servant Jonathan said.

The little monk asked for water. The leader poured a tin cup full—so full the water splashed over the sides. It felt good spilling across the little monk's grayish face. Then it ran down cheeks and chin as firm as unformed clay, finally settling into sweaty puddles in the loose folds of his neck.

"Tell me your dreams," the leader said, wanting to be of help.

"It was nothing," said the little monk.

"It was everything," the leader said with authority. "Never dismiss your dreams. God speaks through dreams. You should always write down your dreams. Put them in your journal. Sometimes a dream is the only way God can get your attention. Our dreams are often letters from God, in one of his many different languages."

The little monk reflected on this and then the whole story of his wrestling with some kind of angelic creature tumbled out.

"What do you make of it?" the little monk inquired, noticing that the leader seemed to be deep in thought.

"First, we must pray," said the leader. The leader went to the door and summoned others to join him in a prayer of healing.

"Will it work?" asked the little monk.

"I can only tell you my experience in a lifetime of offering the prayer of healing. I have prayed for some and they still died. I have prayed for a few who have been dramatically healed. I have prayed for many who have been helped in some way, however small. For some it has taken only one prayer of healing; for most it has taken a series of healing prayer over time; for an unusual few, it has taken concentrated, continuous prayer without ceasing," the leader instructed.

"What can I expect?" the little monk asked.

"I think yours will take a lot of prayer and a long, long time," the leader answered.

A holy calm, a cleansing stillness filled the room.

"Let's do it," affirmed the little monk.

The leader leaned over the little monk and put a hand on his chest and heart, while the little monk, in sad whispers, confessed all his sins. The leader then said a prayer of pardon. He took a vial of oil and spilled a few drops on his fingertips. With those few drops, the leader placed his hand on the little monk's forehead, saying, "I anoint you with oil as an invitation to the Holy Spirit to heal you. Hear our prayer, O God, in the name of the Father and of the Son and of the Holy Spirit."

All those assembled gently placed their hands on the little monk. The leader touched the little monk's heart and then his thigh. The little monk felt a sudden warmth, like an aged wine that sends hot tingles clear to the fingertips. Then he released a deep sigh of peace.

"Do you remember these words of Julian of Norwich?"

Jonathan asked: 'And so our good Lord answered to all the questions and doubts which I could raise, saying most comfortingly: I will make all things well, and I can make all things well, and I shall make all things well, and I will make all things well; and you will see yourself that every kind of thing will be well.'"

"All is well," said the little monk, tucking a blanket around himself, remembering, too, words written long ago by the prophet Isaiah, "Tell the just ones, all is well."

"Now, describe your dream to me," the leader requested.

The little monk offered the details of the dream as well as he could remember them.

"What do you think it all means?" pondered the little monk.

"It means you're a brother to Jacob," explained Servant Jonathan. "You wrestled with an angel as he did. Your hip is out of joint just like his. And ... and you will still have that limp for the rest of your life," Jonathan observed.

"But I got this limp from being jostled by a runaway horse," the little monk argued, "not from an angel."

"Yes, but in your dream, the angel, too, touched your thigh as a sign. You have received a divine wounding," the leader announced.

"A divine wounding? What's that?" inquired the little monk.

"Sometimes, when God deals with a soul in a great way he leaves behind a sign of that dealing as a remembrance to the recipient, but also to the world. The great apostle Paul said, 'The wound which you bear in God's way brings a change of heart too good to regret; but the wound which is borne in the world's way brings death.'"

The little monk was awed that God would choose him to bear a divine wounding.

"There's a deep lesson here—a secret at the heart of the universe," Jonathan added. "My prayer is often this: 'O

God, always leave me lame enough, weak enough, that I must lean on thee.'

"Remember what Isaiah prophesied of the Messiah," remarked Servant Jonathan. "'It was the will of God to bruise him.' Even Jesus himself received a divine wounding, and by his wounds we ourselves are healed."

"You really think I have a divine wounding?" asked the little monk. "What will happen to me?"

"Your limp will linger forever. But the real wound will be in your inmost being. The visible wound is only a symbol of the invisible wound of the soul. Sister Teresa of Avila put it best. She said that in the far recesses of the interior castle where naked soul meets holy God, the pain reaches to the soul's very depths and that when God pulls out the arrow from the wound it is as if God, in love, is drawing our very depths after him."

Jonathan continued, "St. John of the Cross understood these things clearly when he said that 'the healing of the wounds of love comes only from him who inflicted the wounds.' So, it is out of our divine wounding that we have something to offer to others. Love sends us out as wounded healers."

Purr came into the room, jumped up on the bed and curled up near the little monk's arm.

"You're tired," the leader finally said and took his leave of the little monk.

The little monk pulled the blanket up under his nose again, sniffled some, coughed his lungs clear and fell away to a gentle sleep, a quiet purring beside him.

The little monk mumbled something in his sleep about being wounded by love, of being killed softly and slowly by tender mercies.

16. The Dazzling Darkness

*A*fter a long, quiet sleep, the terrible dreams started again. Ugly creatures, smelling of hell, pursued him. Finally, the terror of abandonment. God slowly turned his back and what little light was left in the monk's heart seemed to be snuffed out. Total darkness. The little monk could feel his soul freezing and his heart turning to ice, while his only thought was to beg God not to leave. He heard the door close and God was gone. "Only in thy light do we have light." He was lost between the planets.

He had fallen into a black hole of separation. He clung to God's grace by a slender thread no bigger than a single strand of a spider's web. But even that was snipped away.

The little monk's only desire was a fully resigned wish to die. Perhaps if he just held his breath, he could end it all. He was so broken that no one could put him back together again. He decided to hold his breath and perhaps end it all. He took one last gulp of air and held it for a long time. Just when he started to turn red in the face, Purr rubbed her whiskers against the little monk's cheek, tickling his resolve. Finally his mouth flew open; he burst out in laughter and gasped for air. He did not have the strength to will his own death. Even that was in the hands of God and a cat. Then he was filled with an incredible thought—God was sovereign, God was all in all, God owned him. In total surrender the little monk fell at the foot of the Cross and was crucified.

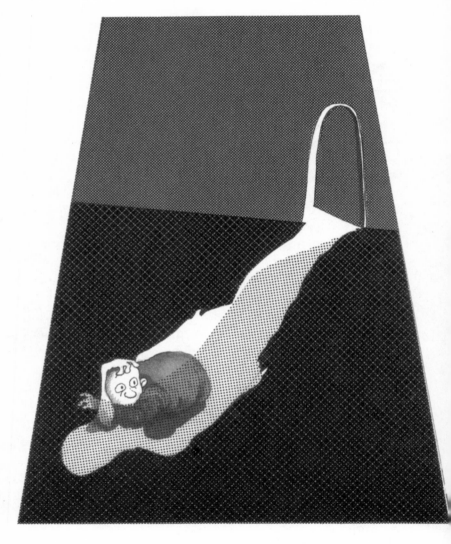

"He heard the door close and God was gone."

He slipped into a dreamy peace, where he walked along pleasant pastures.

A long shadow of love cast itself over the dark room where the stilled body of the little monk lay.

He slept for several days. Then he was stirred by the bleating of sheep and the "baa" of a lamb's voice floating on the morning air. When he finally awakened, Sister Anne was singing a lovely psalm—"from everlasting to everlasting, thou art God."

The rock-heavy weight of sickness had rolled away.

"My, you've had a long nap," Sister Anne said cheerfully.

The little monk blushed to be so taken care of by another human being. He had great difficulty accepting this. He was not one to impose himself on others.

"Something came for you the other day, but I'm afraid it got broken in the transporting," remarked Sister Anne. She took a package from a rough pine table in the corner of the unadorned room. She pulled away the wrapping to reveal a clay vase, now cracked and broken.

The little monk was astonished. He recognized the vase. It was the first good vase he had made when he was an apprentice to the potter. The gentleman who bought it had died, so said an attached note, and left instructions in his will for the vase to be returned to the artist who created it, wherever he might be found. The rest of the note with the vase read: "Thank you for bringing such beauty to my life."

The little monk took the broken sections of vase, as if they were the pieces of his own life. He promised himself that one day he would mend the vase, but for now he would keep the vase as a sign of his own brokenness. Each day he looked at the vase and handled the broken pieces. Then he made this prayer, "O God, Eternal Potter, I've been in your furnace too long. The fire may burn away too much, so that there's nothing left of use even to you."

Deep calling to deep, the little monk prayed for a path through his illness. Soon he was able to be taken to the chapel, a building whose appointments all directed the soul to God. How he loved the holiness of that chapel, filled with sun-splintering stained-glass windows and vivid etchings in stone and wood—a panorama of Redemption's story, a ladder for the soul to climb to God.

One day as he sat there soaking in the beauty of the sacred place, and listening to the singing fill the air, the little monk began to leaf through his journal to find a particular notation regarding the words of St. Augustine. And there it was just as the little monk had written it years ago: "Those who have sung have prayed twice."

He loved the feel of the journal's pages, the look of ordered words as they recorded his inner life. Rereading what he had written always brought a sense of renewal as he gleaned the thoughts and feelings stored throughout his journal.

An early spiritual director, with a touch of humor, once told the little monk, "Always keep a journal. Then if the world ever accuses you of being a saint, your journal will prove them wrong!"

Life went on in the monastery at Maloo. Almost a year later, measured in a monastery not by clicks of the clock, but by the great seasons of the church—Advent, Christmas, Epiphany, Lent, Easter, Ascension, Pentecost, and Kingdomtide—the little monk was able to return to work and gradually resume his duties in the full strength of a summer faith. Memories as glorious as country gardens replaced the fading images of unearned agony.

17. Proceeding with the Will of God

One day as he returned from the forest with his bag of seeds, startling news met him: Servant Jonathan, full of years and the bounty of God, had died during the night. In the leader's lifeless hand was a letter to be opened that afternoon.

The brothers gathered together in the great hall and read the letter aloud. It simply said: "I must be about my Father's other business now. Love each other as much as I have loved you. Your new leader will be the little monk. He will teach you to pray. We shall all meet again in that place where prayer will no longer be needed, but where praise will be eternal."

The little monk fell on his knees and begged God, "Please don't give me the burden of leadership."

When the little monk arose from prayer, a voice within seemed to say: "It is enough that you have been chosen. Do not look for reasons. There are many questions for which there are no earthly answers. To all these questions, we may not ever know the answers this side of death. On the other side of death we will not care about the answers to our questions. We will be with the Savior. That is enough. God is enough. He is the one who fills all things with himself. He is far greater than all our questions or the answers to them."

*"In the leader's lifeless hand was a letter
to be opened that afternoon."*

The little monk touched his injured hip. A sharp twinge shot through him and he felt the Divine Wounding again.

The piling up of days, months and years in learning one prayer lesson a year, but knowing that lesson deep in the bones, shaped the little monk so that he taught with an authority that comes from unshakable confidence in God and profound acceptance of the goodness of each day.

The little monk's counsel became well known.

People from all over came to see him. In many ways they found nothing new in his teaching, except that it had the stamp of authenticity on it, the kind that comes from deep hurt, long suffering and the rich confidence that comes from allowing God to rule one's days. Only those who have been under the surgeon's knife can speak from experience about agony and grace.

Time, who steals from all of us, had no power over the little monk. While the monastery's clock marked holy time, the village's clock measured ordinary time. But the little monk had learned that those who live in God hear both of them as one redeeming cosmic tick.

18. The Bird That Shook
a Kingdom

Smoke, fire and ashes quickly settled over the sleepy expanse around Maloo. The village awoke early one morning to a towering inferno—the monastery!

A young barn swallow had been building her first nest. She picked up a piece of smoldering straw from a leftover fire and flew it to her nest under an eave of the monastery.

Soon the whole nest was ablaze and spread to the monastery itself. A ferocious flame attacked the monastery with an uncontrollable fury. A mighty wind fanned the flames until they danced wildly in the morning dawn.

By the time help arrived, one whole wing had burned, scorched into ruins. Nothing remained but some piles of stone at the four corners. Charred beams formed skeleton silhouettes against the fiery red canopy of heaven. Bushes around the foundations became burning balls of glowing orange.

The day was filled with on-going terror and heroism. Three of the monks had been trapped in a blazing backdraft that roared down the hallways. They were saved only by jumping from the windows, but suffered serious injuries and burns in the process.

Only later, after rescuing two others, did the little monk realize that he had burned his own hands. The palms were blistered a sickly purple with crimson pockets at the centers.

"One whole wing had burned, scorched into ruins..."

Prayer swept the village clean. No heart was untouched. Young people stood paralyzed. Old people busied themselves with small routine tasks. Even stray dogs lay listlessly in pools of their own sadness. Flowers tilted their heads and dimmed their colors in honor of those who rode chariots of fire that day. Trees were too frightened to move their leaves. Forest animals hid in the farthest corners of their homes.

When the whole story unfolded, it became obvious some of the monks would have to move elsewhere until that part of the monastery was rebuilt. Ordinary people in abundance opened their humble dwellings to them and put an extra plate on their meager tables.

And so it was that the little monk was driven by the Spirit into the marketplace and into the homes of common folk. He sat at their dinner tables and washed himself in their oak tubs. Children were asked to give up their beds to him and to double up with their brothers and sisters.

From that experience of living with the ordinary people of this world came numerous stories, proverbs, sayings and wise insights, repeated a thousand times in a thousand ways. Such happenings were quietly whispered over back fences, at the community well, and in the small shops of the village. The stories of the little monk were so passionately told, whispered and gossiped about by the townspeople, that the stories easily and quickly took on the form and power of gospel truth.

Like crumbs from a poor man's table, the sayings of the little monk were gathered up with grateful hearts and stored away for leaner times. Some of that wisdom is shared in the pages that follow. From letters and diaries of people who knew the little monk, these vignettes are offered.

19. Learning How To Pray

A large group of villagers gathered one day to ask the little monk to teach them about the riches of prayer. They were an undisciplined group. They also brought their children with them. Even a few stray dogs from the village joined the group, barking and snipping at each other. Three of the dogs fought each other for a leftover bone, while others gobbled up some crusts from yesterday's bread thrown their way.

"Little monk, teach us all you know about prayer," pleaded the villagers.

The little monk, moved by their desire to learn "the great secret," began at the beginning.

"In order to pray, here is what you should do," the little monk taught. "Say this: 'Our Father, who art in heaven, hallowed be thy name. Thy kingdom come, thy will be done, on earth as it is in heaven. Give us this day our daily bread. And forgive us our trespasses as we forgive those who trespass against us. And lead us not into temptation. But deliver us from evil. For thine is the kingdom, and the power, and the glory, for ever and ever. Amen.'"

"No, no you don't understand," cried the villagers. "We know we *ought* to pray."

"Then you do pray?" asked the little monk.

"Well, yes, sometimes, well, sort of."

"Then, in order to learn *to pray*, begin the day, and each hour thereafter, with the Lord's Prayer. When that has become a habit, you will soon find yourself praying all the time."

A few villagers left, deciding that the little monk had nothing new to offer about the subject of prayer.

"What we really wanted was some simple methods that wouldn't be too hard to do," one of the remaining villagers said. "We want to know *how* to pray."

"In order to learn *how* to pray," the little monk suggested, "Say, 'Our Father, who art in heaven, hallowed be thy name. Thy kingdom come, thy will be done ... '"

"No, no," a villager interrupted. "We know the Lord's Prayer. Now teach us really how to pray, some kind of formula or plan. I don't think you're understanding what we want."

"That is how to pray. That is the plan. That is the discipline. Begin the day, and each hour thereafter, with the Lord's Prayer, and you will know *how* to pray."

Several more villagers left, feeling that the little monk had no depth to his teachings on prayer. He had nothing new. He only taught them what they had been taught from childhood.

"Let me tell you a parable," the little monk said.

"Three people were each given a choice of books to make them wise. One asked for a book on how to make money. Another selected a book of philosophy. The third preferred a book on prayer. Ten years later, the one who chose the book on making money was rich. The second who took the book on philosophy was sought after as a new guru. He traveled worldwide, wrote popular books and had a great following. The one who chose the book on prayer was neither rich nor sought after. Which one of these people was wise?"

Sensing that this might be a trick question, a lawyer answered, "We don't know. Tell us, who was the wise person?"

"They were all wise," answered the little monk. "The

rich man was wise in his own eyes. The philosopher was wise in the sight of others. The man of prayer was wise in the sight of God. Therefore choose your wisdom wisely. Prayer is always the better investment."

Those who stayed gave it one more try. "Little monk, we simply want to know the substance of prayer, the content of prayer, the themes that most please God."

"Oh. I see now," said the little monk. "In order to learn *what* to pray for, say, 'Our Father, who art in heaven, hallowed be thy name. Thy kingdom come, thy will be done, on earth....'"

"No, no," they said, frustrated that they couldn't make the little monk understand.

"But, if you pray that way, begin each day, and each hour thereafter, with the Lord's Prayer, you will know what ought to be the content of true prayer," he answered.

At this, most of the rest of the group left, disgruntled, shaking their heads that the little monk could not grasp the issue.

Finally, the little monk looked out into only two sets of eyes. Everyone else had gone. Remembering the promise that, where two or three are gathered together, Christ is in the midst, the little monk opened his heart and taught the fullness of prayer, beginning with the gaze of God and ending with the prayer of intercession. He stared far into the depths of those two sets of eyes and taught with great intensity.

The little monk led them in this simple prayer:

Lord, you are our stillpoint.
    We are here.
    You are here.
    We are where we are supposed to be,
        for we are at the center of our beginnings.
                                    Amen.

The little monk concluded his teaching and thanked the two who had stayed to the end. Then they both walked off slowly and silently toward home, a young boy and his dog.

The little monk prayed: "Dear Father, chisel again deeply the letters on my epitaph, lest I forget that I once died to the world."

He headed down the road, stopping long enough to inspect a split sycamore tree, struck by lightning the night before.

"The little monk concluded his teaching…"

20. The Sage

*I*n a debate one day, when asked why Jesus was crucified, the little monk answered: "Because he asked too many questions."

A young man inquired of the little monk, "Why does the devil hate my father so much?" The little monk answered: "Because God took away his anger long ago and the devil no longer has a door into his life."

A businessman once came to the little monk by night to discuss money. "I love money," he confessed to the little monk. "That's because you have no person to love," answered the little monk. "What do you mean?" asked the businessman. "Greed is the absence of someone to love," said the little monk. "Find someone to love and you'll no longer worship money."

A dwarf came to the little monk to ask why he, the dwarf, had been made so ugly by the creator. "He made you in his image," said the little monk. The dwarf was shocked that the little monk would think of God as ugly. "Perhaps God isn't ugly," the little monk responded. "But if the worldly ones can assume that God is beautiful like them, then we who are poor, ugly, and broken can just as easily assume that God is like us, for the Scriptures bear that out."

A villager said to the little monk: "My neighbor slapped me. Should I forgive him?" "Yes," answered the little monk. "How many times should I forgive my neighbor?" the villager asked. "How many times did he slap you?"

asked the little monk. "Once," came the answer. "Then forgive him once," said the little monk. "But what if he slaps me fifty times?" the villager asked. "Then you should forgive him forty-nine times," came the answer. "Why only forgive forty-nine times, when I was struck fifty times?" the villager asked. The little monk: "Freely accept the fiftieth slap. You deserved it for being such a fool to allow yourself to be slapped the first forty-nine times."

One harvest-moon night a rich man found the little monk scanning the skies. "Who owns the stars?" the man asked. "I do," answered the little monk. "Isn't that selfish, to own stars?" the man asked. "Not if I give them away," responded the little monk. The man: "But why would you give them away?" The little monk: "So others can own them for a while. All of us should own the stars at least some time in our life."

The little monk was known far and wide for some of his proverbs: "A bird in the hand is an awful responsibility." "Time is the interval between two prayers." "Evil is good overdone." "Bees know what they're doing and so do apples and monkeys. Why are we so lost for purpose?"

Two skeptics followed the little monk home one day, challenging him about doctrine. One of the skeptics asked: "Why is the Incarnation of Christ so important?" Little monk: "Because people could see Christ's shadow. Beware of the god who casts no shadow."

A seeker once pleaded: "Teach me the essence of the Gospels, please." The little monk responded: "The Gospel of Matthew shows us the value of order. The Gospel of Mark shows us the power of action. The Gospel of Luke shows us the need for wholeness and the Gospel of John shows us the love of God. That's the Gospel: Order, Action, Wholeness, Love."

Of all the strange people who sought out the little monk, none provided a more unusual visit than that of a thief.

The thief: "I came to tell you that I am the greatest thief in the world." He then named three famous robberies, all known to the little monk. "Why are you telling me this?" asked the little monk. "Because I wanted to get it off my chest and tell someone. You being a religious man, however, can't report me." The little monk: "But God heard you, too, and he's not very good at keeping secrets."

A political leader: "What was the hardest thing that ever happened to you?" The little monk: "Dethronement!" Political leader: "I never knew you were a king." Little monk: "I wasn't, but I acted as if I were." Political leader: "What happened?" Little monk: "I met Christ on the road one day, and he bowed down before me. I said, 'Lord, what are you doing?' He answered, 'There can be only one Lord of the Universe and yet there are two on the road today. Since there can be only one king, I decided to step down.' Needless to say, my own personal kingdom collapsed that day and now I serve a new king."

A villager: "Why do you spend so much time with animals?" Little monk: "The Scriptures tell me that Christ is an eagle, a lion, and a lamb. How will I know what that means unless I spend time with them?"

A desperate seeker: "What is peace, anyway?" The little monk: "Peace is a prayer on the lips and a cat in the lap."

"How can one live again, after one has been betrayed?" asked a young woman whose husband had divorced her. The deep hurt showed in her eyes. Little monk: "You must list all of the feelings you have: hurt, anger, unworthiness, lovelessness, desire for revenge, never wanting to trust again, and then find a nail on Jesus' cross on which to hang each hurt. He, too, was betrayed beyond measure. Soon you will see that each and every one of your wounds perfectly matches the wounds of Christ."

One looking for greater discipline: "Can you give me a

rule of life?" The little monk: "I can only tell you mine. It serves me well, but may kill you. My rule of life is:

to win my world to a sense of wonder,
to spoil my world with small decencies,
to color my world brightly with endless splashes of beauty,
to ruin my world's standards by always living out my baptism,
to surprise my world with unexpected kindnesses,
to fill my world with the incense of undeserved love,
to teach my world a more excellent way,
to startle my world with good news,
to listen deeply in a shallow world,
to pray without ceasing and...
to never let life end with 'uh-oh,' for that would mean being unprepared."

A dying brother asked the little monk, "What is the greatest Scripture text ever written on the subject of death?" Little monk: "Unless a grain of wheat falls to the earth and dies, it remains just a grain of wheat. But if it dies, it produces much fruit." Dying brother: "But I have heard all that before." Little monk: "Yes, but now you can experience it. Let me know how it comes out." Dying brother: "But how will it come out?" Little monk: "That's the last lesson on earth and the first lesson of eternity."

Often when asked to be taught what he knew about the mysteries of the kingdom, he would hand the person a bag of sea shells. "All that I know is already written in the stories of these shells," he would say as he walked off, expecting the person to study hard the intricate patterns and varied shapes of the shells. Most returned the bag unopened, but a few did become disciples of those shells—gifts from the sea—and found in them infinite parables of life.

21. The Responsibility of Glory

*T*he little monk loved to look back and remember the very first day he had arrived at the monastery. How he had loved its austere beauty, its enticing intimacy, its rhythmic power as the hours of the day were marked out for prayer and reflection.

The little monk was growing older in body but younger in spirit. He appreciated the beauty of God's world with all of his heart and with all of the wonder of a child.

The well where he often went for prayer held sweet memories for him. He dropped a stone into its emptiness and heard the reassuring and familiar splash call out to him.

A speckled hen crossed his path in search of lost grain that may have fallen by the wayside. The little monk looked at the hen intently, studying her meaning. She, too, is part of the fullness of creation, he reflected. His thoughts continued: Every creature is part of God's plan and rule, whether it be a sparrow, an ox or a rhinoceros. All of creation, to the last lily of the field, praise God by being what they are. Just as the hand cannot say to the foot, "I have no need of you," neither can we say, even to a speckled hen, clucking for food on a dusty road, "The world would be better without you."

He took out his journal, dusted it off, and turned to

what he had written that first day when he gave his heart
to the monastery at Maloo.

"This is the place where God dwells. Even the dirt that
squishes between my toes is sacred ground," he had written. Then he added a tenth century prayer by Manchan of
Liath:

I wish, O Son of the living God, ancient eternal King,
for a secret hut in the wilderness that it may be my
dwelling.

A very blue shallow well to be beside it, a clear pool
for washing away sins through the grace of the Holy
Ghost.

A beautiful wood close by around it on every side,
for the nurture of many-voiced birds, to shelter and
hide it.

Facing the south for warmth, a little stream across its
enclosure, a choice ground with abundant bounties
which would be good for every plant.

A few sage disciples, I will tell their number, humble
and obedient, to pray to the King.

Four threes, three fours, fit for every need, two sixes
in the church both south and north.

Six couples in addition to me myself, praying
through the long ages to the King who moves the
sun.

A lovely church decked with linen, a dwelling for

God of Heaven; then, bright candles over the holy white Scriptures.

One room to go to for the care of the body, without wantonness, without voluptuousness, without meditation of evil.

This is the housekeeping I would undertake. I would choose it without concealing: fragrant fresh leeks, hens, speckled salmon, bees.

My fill of clothing and of food from the King of good frame, and for me to be sitting for a while praying to God in every place.

The little monk's face glowed as he reveled in the joy of those days and in the splendors of steadfastness. "Dear Father," prayed the little monk, "I have not hurried away from being a shepherd after thee."

While his mind fondled the golden memories that surrounded this place which had been home for him for so many years, he heard the brothers singing a psalm:

"How lovely are Thy dwelling places, O Lord of
    hosts!
My soul longed and even yearned for the courts of
    the Lord;
My heart and my flesh sing for joy to the living God.
The bird also has found a house,
And the swallow a nest for herself, where she may
    lay her young,
Even Thine altars, O Lord of hosts,
My King and my God.
How blessed are those who dwell in Thy house!
They are ever praising Thee."

He thought of the swallow nesting with her young on the very altar of God. Our heavenly Father always provides, he affirmed.

"I must find another leader for my brothers," whispered the little monk to Purr. "It is time for me to share the secrets of leadership."

A short time later one of the monks startled the little monk as his mind floated on a sea of holy memories. "Little monk," he said, touching his shoulder, "it's time for our meeting."

The meeting, usually a very brief time to get the group together to handle items of a more "business" nature, took a dramatic turn. There was a letter from the bishop. The little monk read it to himself first, choking back confused feelings, before he read it aloud to the group. The bishop was closing the monastery at Maloo and transferring the remaining members to another monastery nearby.

"I'm sending you as a group to another monastery for further training for a while," the bishop wrote. "Then you will be scattered like seed, for the kingdom of God is like a newly-plowed farm. Each of you will be planted in other soil, for no sower sows all his seed in one place, but casts it against the wind, letting the wind blow it where it will. God has made you dancers in the desert, musicians in a silent night and artists of colorless lives. God prepared for you a lavish banquet in a famined land, a bountiful table in the wilderness. Soon he will send you forth to spread the fire of Maloo."

The group was stunned by the news. Maloo was to close! Beautiful, cherished Maloo was to end and pass into history. The monks were to begin their journey to the new monastery sometime in the next few weeks, as soon as they could put things in order for the move.

There was a separate note from the bishop, for the little monk's eyes only. "Little monk, although the others are being sent to another monastery, I'm asking you to come and spend some time with me. My health is failing and I will not be able to continue much longer. I have been pleased with your progress in prayer. But there are a few things I would still like to share with you about the power of prayer. True prayer has much to commend it, especially if it can take one even through the darkness of death into the land of endless light. You will remain for a while at Maloo, alone, until you understand all that Maloo means. Then come to me with haste. Come before winter, at the latest. Your presence will be of great comfort to me. Do you still have that cat with you? Bring her, too. Perhaps petting her will ease my shaking hand. Pray for me, little monk."

He thought of the first day the bishop had singled him out in the great cathedral and of the curious map the bishop had drawn for him of how to get to Maloo. The little monk had decided long ago that the map was a kind of spiritual game the bishop often played with those who took him too seriously for their own good. He took out a few seeds, blew them into the wind and then brought his bishop before the throne of God in prayer.

These pleasant memories were shattered by the brothers who began to argue among themselves. They were obligated to obey the bishop, yet the decision to close Maloo seemed to be in opposition to what Maloo stood for. Certainly they had all taken vows of poverty, stability, purity and obedience, but they had also learned that the call to obedience and submission to a superior was the most difficult of the four vows.

As their leader, the little monk spoke his mind on the matter.

"Listen to this parable," he said quietly.

"A king had two sons. They were brought before him so that he could admire them. 'I love you,' he said to the one

"He took out a few seeds and blew them into the wind…"

son. The son answered, 'And I love you, too, Father.' The king was very pleased by his son's response and replied, 'Then go to the stables and clean the horses' stalls and scatter the dung on the garden.' The son nodded but did not do it.

"The king said to the second son, 'I love you,' to which the son replied nothing. The king then commanded him to go to the stables and clean the horses' stalls and scatter the dung on the garden. The son went and did as he was told. Then the king said, 'Proclaim throughout the land that I have a son who loves me.'"

"What does this parable mean?" asked one of the brothers.

"It means that obedience is love," replied the little monk.

"Know this," added the little monk. "You will all be sorely pressed to find the will of God. You will have to determine whether the voice you hear speaking in you is the voice of self, the voice of Satan, or the voice of the Savior. This will be an arduous battle for spiritual discernment."

They decided to take a three day vow of silence to listen for the voice of God.

A timeless quiet shrouded the monastery.

It was quiet, that is, until the earthquake came rumbling through the mountains and shook the desert floor. The earthquake cracked the chapel. The walls, like curtains, opened to the outside.

No one was injured. Also, none could miss that this was possibly a divine sign, a speaking of God. Their calling was decided.

The little monk did something he had not done in a very long time. He pulled himself into his robe, as he used to do as a young monk in order to disappear from the world and "center down" into the presence of God. He found a worthy spot in a corner of the old rose garden, now turned to thorns, weeds, and wormwood. He stayed there through most of the night.

He had a growing uneasiness about himself. And it had nothing, in a sense, to do with the bishop's order to close the monastery. Something deeper, more personal plagued him. It came down to this—he felt wearied of this world and longed eagerly for the next. How he wished for a chariot of fire to take him home.

At one point, he looked up and searched the night sky for perhaps a comet, but saw none.

Yet something welled up within him: the Holy Spirit was about to do something new with him. When one becomes a good friend to the Holy Spirit, one will always live in the glory of great expectations, he concluded.

22. A New Chariot

*T*he day began as usual with a liturgy of cheerful birds high up in the trees. A bell rang softly on the morning air. It would sound no more for Maloo.

When the brothers met, the little monk somehow seemed to have grown even more wise. His eyes, they noticed, were compelling. The little monk's eyes glowed with rings of shimmering fire on the outer edges and pools of molten crystal farther in.

All of the brothers were of one accord. God had spoken the same message to each of them: they were to accept the mandate of the bishop to leave Maloo and move as one to a new monastery. The little monk agreed. There seemed to be great relief that they were all of one mind and spirit.

"I will not be going with you, though," announced the little monk, to the amazement of the brothers.

"Yes, but God has spoken and told us to leave," said one.

"Yes, yes," the others agreed.

"I know," said the little monk. "But my work is different from yours at this time." His eyes sparkled with earnestness. "I am not to go to the new monastery. The bishop has called me. I am to return home. The time will come soon enough, though, that I must be about my Father's other business and join Servant Jonathan and Sister Anne in an even grander work, for heaven is the last great monastery of all, you know. You are to go ahead. I am to wait at Maloo a little longer and then go to the bishop."

A sweet sadness filled the busy days as the brothers prepared to leave. Early one morning before daybreak, they shared a final breakfast together. After morning prayer, they went out to the waiting wagons. Purr paced worriedly at all the activity. Then for a time, she lay in the middle of the road. Finally she sauntered over to one of the wagons, unsure of whether she was to go or stay.

After numerous farewells, nothing remained but awkward silence. The brothers climbed into the wagons and pulled away slowly. To wave goodbye to the little monk, to leave behind their friend and companion, pained them greatly. Yet, as their weather-battered wagon rounded the bend in the road, some of the pain was eased by the excitement of what was to be, and that filled them with hope.

They looked back a final time to see the little monk, but he was only a shadow in the dust.

They would miss their friend. Their *two* friends, in fact, for Purr would also be sorely missed.

Some legends say that flowers bloomed in the desert wherever their tears fell on the journey away from Maloo.

Now alone, the little monk turned to sorting out his own thoughts and feelings about the meaning of Maloo.

Why had the bishop been persuaded that the little monk would become a great voice of prayer at Maloo, when God seemed to be saying that now there would not be time for that? This, more than anything else, puzzled the little monk. There was nothing to do except to listen to the voice that seemed to be speaking so clearly in his heart and mind. He knew it would be some days before he returned to the bishop. There was still something that needed to be finished here.

But who would be here to carry on the gospel of prayer? He could only trust in a faithful God. His fear dissolved as he prayed, "O God, make me as faithful to you as you have been to me. Help me, God, to bring into focus what my life will mean to others after I have gone."

The desert seemed to sense that he was alone now and more vulnerable. Sandstorms came often, wind-blown grains of merciless sand scraping at his skin.

Finally, one day he went to the chapel and knelt to pray. Purr followed loyally along behind him.

Afterward he wrote in his journal: "Many people approach God with great feeling, with joy, tears and sorrow. Some want an emotionally charged experience with God. Many come with images and pictures in their minds of a visual God. Some come with their minds filled with great thoughts of God. And there is a side of God which is revealed to those who seek him these ways. He will always enter and dine with those who seek him: 'Behold I stand at the door and knock. If any man will open the door, I will come in and banquet with him.' "

He ended his journal there. The book was full from cover to cover.

The little monk pulled his robe around him and his hood up over his head. As best he could, he sank into the robe, as he used to do, and lost himself in this quiet request. "Help me to find some worthy person to continue my work in prayer."

He thought of the words of St. Augustine and heartily agreed, "Late have I loved you, O beauty, so ancient and so new, late have I loved you." This was the meaning of Maloo.

Suddenly, the little monk felt a new stirring of life. His heart soared like an eagle. He instinctively knew that his prayers were about to be answered.

A soft, wordless voice whispered a great promise to him:

"You have spent a lifetime trying to grasp things by the clumsy tool of human-sense perceptions. You will go beyond this and experience and discover a side of God few ever know."

What a strange promise, he thought. Yet he laughed the laughter of Abraham and Sarah, first in disbelief, and then in wonderment at the sovereign promise of God.

He knew it was time to leave Maloo and return home. But he would not need the journal now, for its secrets were in his heart and God was holding out still another challenge. He would leave the journal with the villagers as their remembrance of the monastery. He gave it to a young mother to hold in trust.

Then he called the children together for a final time of play. Afterward he gave them gifts: small bags of seeds, pretty stones from the stream, a favorite clay pot, sea-worn shells, a loaf of spiced bread, and a slingshot.

He left Maloo the next day at dawn, never looking back, for he now realized that Maloo was not a specific locale, but a place in the heart. Maloo, he concluded, is Passion, Easter and Pentecost all rolled into one holy, inner feast that you can celebrate in your heart wherever you are.

"Come, Purr, old friend, let's get this 'chariot' moving," he said. With Purr snuggled on his lap, he peacefully headed the horse and wagon off in the direction of the morning star.

"Afterwards he gave them gifts..."

23. The Boy Who Set Fires

Years later, a few families from the village decided to move elsewhere to improve their financial lot. They packed up their possessions, wagon following wagon. Since it was late in the day they decided to camp at the old monastery before moving on.

"Keep your eye on that boy," the wagonmaster said to his wife. The wagonmaster—like his father and his grand-father before that—was a blacksmith by trade, hammering out all sorts of things from hot iron. He was tall, strong, proud and accustomed to plain living, high thinking and keen observing. He had hoped that his son would carry on the family trade.

His son was fifteen and the blight of his life. If there was any trouble to get into, this boy did it: stealing, rebel-lion, running away, drinking and partying, as well as chasing the girls. He had been arrested several times for drunkenness and fighting. He was a solid, muscular youth with an arrogant face and clay-gray, piercing eyes—a bully of bullies. He had an angry heart that always leaned in the direction of trouble.

The villagers suspicioned him and a friend of setting numerous fires in the area. Nothing was ever proved, but his mother knew in her heart that he was guilty, no matter how much he denied setting the fires. She came to one tragic scene in which seven show horses were destroyed in a terrible barn fire. Her son and his friend were already there, watching and listening to the sad whinnies of the dying horses. Although his mother wept despairingly, the young boy and his friend shed not a single tear, nor showed any sign of remorse or regret.

"How can you not weep for such tragedy?" she asked them.

"They're not my horses," her son responded coldly.

Now that they were leaving Maloo, his mother was glad to have a new start, if only she could keep her son out of trouble. But in spite of her husband's warning and her own watchful eye, the boy was able to sneak off from camp. He took a whiskey bottle with him and hid out in the chapel at Maloo.

After a long time, his mother found him—and he was drunk.

"You must be very lonely. Those who live in rebellion always have hearts full of loneliness. Some say that people are lonely and troubled because they build barricades rather than bridges," she said. The boy took another drink from his bottle. He stared at her in disbelief that she could be so simple-minded.

"But what do *you* say, mother?" asked the boy.

"Your pain is definitely from the loneliness of evil that surrounds you," she said sorrowfully. "But there is also a good loneliness that comes from God. I heard this from a little monk who lived here for many years. As he left, he handed me his most treasured possession, this book. He said it was about inwardness and being alone with God, but never being really alone as we know it."

And his mother handed him a tattered book—it looked like someone's journal—clearly worn by years and years of use.

"Inwardness? Alone with God?" he asked, puzzled by such words.

By the light of a single candle glowing in the darkness of the chapel, he read far into the night about a life that he

"After a long time, his mother found him…and he was drunk."

wanted with all of his being. He cupped his hands around the candle for a little warmth against the night. An owl hooted in the distance and the forest moaned softly. From time to time, black vultures, roosting in the rafters of the old chapel, cast their shadows down over him.

He awoke the next morning to his father's voice. "You miserable thing," his father screamed and then slapped his face. "We are ready to leave this wretched place and you are nowhere to be found." The boy turned red with anger and was ready to strike back.

Instead, the words of the book he was holding captured his heart. When holding these treasures of the kingdom he could not muster any hatred.

"I'm sorry, Father," said the boy, hiding the book from his father's searching eyes.

"Get in the wagon. We're leaving this worthless ruin. There's nothing of value here for us."

His father started to swing his hand back to slap the boy again. But seeing a determination in his son that he had never seen before, he only pushed the boy to the waiting wagon.

The caravan traveled for several months in its journey from Maloo to other worlds. All in the caravan noticed the change in the boy.

He seemed silent, distracted, gathered into his own thoughts and often seeking solitude. Several times people were startled by coming upon him kneeling in prayer, tears gushing from a deep well within him. There was no doubt about it. There was something in that strange book he was reading that was transforming him. People whispered and gossiped in amazement that such a rebel—like a wayward, stubborn lamb—should have fallen prey to the Lion in the wilderness.

Yet, when asked about the book he would only mention

something about living in the presence of Christ—a pris-
oner to the highest majesty.

Later, when the teachings of the book had deeply
formed him spiritually, he was often heard to witness that
"The little monk says this," or "The journal says that."

He would note something like, "Listen to this. Listen to
what the journal says: 'You can be truly converted only in
silence. That's where God will meet you—in silence and
solitude.' " Or he might offer, "The little monk wrote this
from one of the saints: 'Keep yourself in peace and you
will convert a thousand souls.' "

People around the countryside never quite got used to
this young boy who often broke into their conversations
with—

"The little monk says ..."